THE
BLUE
JEANS
GOSPEL

THE
BLUE JEANS GOSPEL

Experiencing
a Real
and Comfortable
Relationship
with Jesus

ROB CRUVER

with DEBRA CRUVER

RIVER GROVE
BOOKS

Published by River Grove Books
Austin, TX
www.rivergrovebooks.com

Distributed by River Grove Books

For ordering information or special discounts for bulk purchases, please contact River Grove Books at PO Box 91869, Austin, TX 78709, 512.891.6100.

Design and composition by Greenleaf Book Group
Cover design by Greenleaf Book Group
Cover image: ©iStock/StudioThreeDots

Cataloging in Publication Data is available.

ISBN: 978-1-63299-043-3

Part of the Tree Neutral® program, which offsets the number of trees consumed in the production and printing of this book by taking pro-active steps, such as planting trees in direct proportion to the number of trees used: www.treeneutral.com

TreeNeutral®

Printed in the United States of America on acid-free paper

15 16 17 18 19 20   10 9 8 7 6 5 4 3 2 1

First Edition

Other Edition(s):
eBook ISBN: 978-1-63299-044-0

To my children. I love you.
May you walk closely with Jesus and always
wear your blue jeans with joy.

CONTENTS

INTRODUCTION

I love blue jeans. They are my wardrobe staple; they define "comfort" for me. I can wear them all day long, then lay them next to the bed at night, and in the morning just put them right back on again. No need to iron them, fold them, or hang them in the closet. They are always ready to go another day. Need washing? Toss them in the laundry and grab another pair. Get ripped? Who cares? People pay extra for rips, frays, and discoloration these days. Jeans are classic and generally timeless. I think jeans look nice with anything from a workout tank to a dress shirt. I wear them pretty much everywhere except to more formal occasions, when I'm inclined to dress for other people and my comfort really isn't a priority.

There's familiarity and comfort that comes with the right pair of jeans once I've been wearing them and wearing them . . . and wearing them. And jeans are durable and generally affordable.

My wife once told me, "Rob, if you ever write a book, it should be about your life in blue jeans." That sparked an idea for this book, although it isn't really much about my life or even that much about blue jeans. The primary element is comfort—something I automatically associate with my jeans, but something people rarely associate with God. I wanted to write about a relationship with God that is real and intimate, even comfortable. That may sound a little bit strange when we are speaking about relating to a Being that is eternal, unlimited, and unequaled. But let's just see how this unfolds. We want to consider finding life's "sweet spot," where we feel and experience the fit of our heart like perhaps we've found in a favorite pair of jeans. I happen to be certain that's the kind of relationship God wants with us, and that's why this book is called *The Blue Jeans Gospel.*

Here are a few core things you should know about me from the start—these are beliefs that shape my every breath: First, I believe that God is real and not just a cultural myth or psychological creation. I also believe that God has revealed himself to us most clearly through Jesus Christ—the fullest and most authentic expression of God. I am further convinced that the documents that comprise what is called the Bible are trustworthy, and accurately express the truth of God and the life and teachings of Jesus. And finally, it is my conviction that only in Jesus are the deepest needs of the human heart met, and only through him can we enter an eternal and intimate relationship with God. Or, as Jesus expressed it himself, "I am the way, the truth, and the life. No one can come to the Father except through me" (John 14:6).

Many other books have been written to argue for or against the kinds of beliefs I have just expressed. Although I have read and pondered a large number of these books, I won't be adding to those arguments in this writing. Instead, I come to you as one who is convinced—intellectually, emotionally, and experientially. It is my heartfelt desire that I, and any who may read this book, move beyond belief into an amazing relationship. According to the teachings of Jesus, God wants us to know him and love him as he knows and loves us.

Thankfully, God is not satisfied with talking weather, politics, or sports (although he may enjoy the sports part). These tend to be our "go to" topics when we aren't interested (or comfortable) in going deeper. But God desires communication on the deepest level, as we enjoy with only our dearest friends and companions.

At the time Jesus entered planet Earth, walking with God had somehow become primarily about rules and regulations. There were all kinds of expectations and checklists that many of us are still bound to today. When we think about God and faith and Christianity, we tend to think about a list of dos and don'ts. We often picture God as a judge, eager to accuse and condemn us for breaking one of his countless rules. Our "religion" is formed out of fear or guilt because we want God to accept us and not be mad at us. I think this kind of faith is tragic, cynical, and even dangerous.

In this book we will consider a different perspective—one in which God actually loves us and wants us to know and obey him because we actually love him. Jesus spoke about and lived out this message clearly and faithfully for us.

In the chapters ahead, we will move deeper into what it looks like to know and love God as well as to grow in a relationship with him that is real, intimate, and life-changing. I break it down into three parts—Loving as Jesus Loved, Living as Jesus Lived, and Serving as Jesus Served—because, by following Jesus's example in these three areas, our lives will settle into a beautiful, meaningful, and intimate relationship with him that will not only change our lives, but impact the people we meet and give us contentment and an assurance that our lives are purposeful and significant.

So go ahead, throw on your most comfortable pair of jeans (or whatever comfort clothes you prefer) and settle down into a cozy chair, because this is about the blue jeans gospel.

Part I

LOVING AS JESUS LOVED

One

...

LOVING GOD

I was in conversation with a friend recently who said, "Please, Rob, please, tell me there's more. Tell me there's more to this Christianity thing than what I see going on in churches or what I see in most people's lives. Tell me there is something more real, more powerful, more intimate that's available than what I've yet experienced. Tell me that it's not just about going to church and performing some religious rituals and calling myself a Christian—tell me there's more!"

So I said, "Okay, there *is* more. There's *a lot* more!"

There's so much more because Jesus says if we remain in him, his Spirit will flow within us. He reveals himself to us in ways that he cannot reveal himself to others. He brings his outrageous joy and peace into our lives. He immerses us in his love and power, and our lives will produce lots of amazing fruit. Yes—there is so much more available (see John 15:5–12).

Back when Jesus showed up on earth, some two thousand–plus years ago, there were all these laws, traditions, and regulations that had accumulated and that determined whether or not someone really measured up and was a follower of God in good standing. It was a standard set way above human ability, and try as they may, everyone failed miserably. Into the midst of this, Jesus entered. He wore regular clothes (no denim back then) and seemed much more focused on heart than behavior, on relationship than regulation.

Jesus's invitation didn't go something like, "Hey I've got this form for you to fill out. I want to know all about your background, including marital and educational status. I'd like to see your financial portfolio. Here are the six hundred and thirteen laws of the Hebrew scriptures. Please check off the laws you've been faithful to and return the forms certified. Once I review these, I'll determine whether we can have a relationship." Thankfully, Jesus doesn't relate to humanity in the manner of a bureaucracy or financial institution.

Instead, Jesus looked people eye-to-eye and went heart-to-heart with a simple and sincere request: "Follow me" (Matthew 4:19; Mark 1:17). Jesus made it clear that he was looking for those who would trust him, be his faithful friends, and walk the dusty roads together with him out of love—not just pressure or fear, or for the sake of appearances.

One day, an expert in religious law came to Jesus and asked, "Teacher, which is the most important commandment in the law of Moses?" (Matthew 22:34–40). He wanted to know the bottom line: What is it that God really, really wants from us? This was a very significant conversation because, as I mentioned, there were 613 laws and commands from the scriptures that had been codified by the religious leaders of Jesus's day. The person asking the question was known as a Pharisee. The Pharisees were the keepers of the law in Israel—the ones who really took it seriously. And this was a very real question, because the Pharisees of this day spent a lot of time discussing it. They would actually gather and debate which laws were greater and which ones were lesser—which ones did God really care about and which ones were kind of extra credit. It was enough to make someone's head spin and heart go numb.

Now, nothing against rules. Rules can give healthy guidelines and let us know where we stand and what is expected of us. There is a measure of comfort and protection and even freedom within boundaries. But when there are so many rules that we become bound up and motionless for fear of breaking one, something is wrong. In John 10:10, Jesus said he came to give people a "rich and satisfying life" (abundant in purpose, meaning, and quality), and I'm certain that didn't mean that we would sit still while holding our breath in fear of breaking his rules.

Jesus answers this Pharisee and essentially says, "You're missing it." Right from the beginning, it's really only ever been about this: "'You must love the your God with all your heart, all your soul, and all your mind.' This is the first and greatest commandment. A second is equally important: 'Love your neighbor as yourself.'" Jesus then said something that blew their minds (and mine): "The entire law and all the demands of the prophets are based on these two commandments" (Matthew 22:36–40; Deuteronomy 6:5; Leviticus 19:18).

What? That's it? Was Jesus serious? Hundreds of laws that took every ounce of energy to even remember, much less keep, and all of them could be summed up by "love"? Could it really be that the core of God's hope and longing for us is fulfilled in truly loving him and truly loving others? Jesus said, "That's it!" That's God's heart from the beginning, and, my friend, God's heart has not changed.

I've been married for twenty-five years to an amazing and beautiful woman. Together we have raised two remarkable children (with only a little heartburn) and have adopted others into our heart and home along the way. Over the years we have journeyed together through a lot of life's ups and downs. When it comes to our relationship, what do you think my wife wants most from me on a daily basis? That I've rinsed my toothpaste down the sink, or that I've returned the toilet seat to its neutral position? These are very helpful and certainly put a smile on her face, but these aren't core to her heart. Perhaps she wants to know that I've been faithful to her with my eyes and my actions? This is extremely important and critical for the health of our relationship, but it's still not sufficient for her deepest heart. Including and beyond these things, what my wife most wants to hear and know on an ongoing basis is that I *love* her.

In the next two chapters, we'll look a bit at what it means to love our neighbor as we love ourselves. But the foundation of it all is having a heart that truly loves God. Our focus should never primarily be about external appearances or behavior. It's always been primarily internal—God has always wanted our hearts and devotion. Anything less than that is like chasing the wind (Ecclesiastes 2:11).

Centuries before Jesus had this conversation with this

religious leader, God spoke through a man named Isaiah. Isaiah was a regular, denim-wearing kind of guy but also a prophet, which simply meant he listened closely to God and shared with others what he heard. And this is what God said to the children of Israel through Isaiah: "These people say they are mine. They honor me with their lips, but their hearts are far from me. And their worship of me is nothing but man-made rules learned by rote" (Isaiah 29:13). Jesus bravely quoted these words in the faces of the religious people of his day (Matthew 15:8). Ouch! I don't think we would ever want to hear God say to us, "You say the right words, you look the part, but your heart isn't anywhere close to what you pretend to be."

The most important commandment of God has never changed. It remains, to love the Lord with all of our heart (emotions, passion, and desires), to love him with all of our soul (this unique and eternal center of our being), and to love him with all of our mind (yes, even our thought processes and the firing of our neurons are to be surrendered to God). God simply wants the whole package of who we are—nothing more, nothing less. This is to be our comfort zone—the sweet spot where we will experience a life that is immeasurably satisfying. God wants it that real, that intimate.

Paul McCartney and the Beatles once summed it

up well: "All you need is love." But it's not a generic, warm-and-fuzzy kind of love. It is a focused, informed, and devoted love. The Greek word for "love" that Jesus uses here is *agape*. This love is self-sacrificing and unconditional. It shows up even when we're not "feeling it," just like Jesus did. This is the real-thing kind of love. It's amazing to be on the receiving end of this, but living it in return will often stretch us. Unlike wearing our favorite pair of jeans, extending real love will not always make us feel comfortable. On the night before Jesus went to the cross, he cried out, "My Father! If it is possible, let this cup of suffering be taken away from me. Yet I want your will to be done, not mine" (Matthew 26:39). Jesus wasn't *comfortable* about going to the cross for us. He did it out of total devotion and self-sacrificing love (agape). Our culture doesn't know much about this kind of love.

As we follow Jesus, we will at times sense and feel his presence, bringing peace and comfort to our hearts. But there will be other times we won't. Life gets hard and sometimes we may feel and say (just like Jesus did), "My God, my God, why have you abandoned me?" (Matthew 27:46). Jesus was not feeling the Father's presence or seeing him in the midst of this storm. But love (agape) moved him forward.

It's always easier for us to keep the emotional kind of

love burning for someone who reaches out in love to us first and who returns our affections. So it's important we understand that God is love and did love us first. Consider these words from John, a real close friend of Jesus, written in 1 John 4:7–10:

> Dear friends, let us continue to love one another, for love comes from God. Anyone who loves is a child of God and knows God. But anyone who does not love does not know God, for God is love. God showed how much he loved us by sending his one and only Son into the world so that we might have eternal life through him. This is real love—not that we loved God, but that he loved us and sent his Son as a sacrifice to take away our sins.

I think it's life-changing when we grasp this concept. Love isn't just something God does, it's who he *is*. Everything that we experience here on earth that is good, kind, and loving flows from God. God created us in love, and when we turned our backs on him, he chose to come to us in love through his Son. And so when God tells us that he wants us to love him with all of our heart and soul and mind—everything that we are—it's because he has loved us that way first. He's simply asking us for a response.

The great challenge, of course, is that our natural heart can be rather selfish—we all tend toward being egocentric. Certainly, we may do some good and even sacrificial things, but in our inner core, even the good that we do is very often more about us. That's why Jesus stepped up and stepped in and offers us new hearts. God promised that a day would come when

> I will give you a new heart, and I will put a new spirit in you. I will take out your stony, stubborn heart, and give you a tender, responsive heart. And I will put my Spirit in you so that you will follow my decrees and be careful to obey my regulations. (Ezekiel 36:26–27)

That's the promise that was fulfilled under the new covenant—meaning a legally binding agreement—between God and man through Jesus. It's pretty amazing. The heart that bows to Jesus will receive God's Spirit. His Spirit will change us from the inside out and give us the power and the desire to want to love him. That's *huge* and exactly what we needed. That's our sweet spot!

I hope we can move beyond some of the religious thoughts and attitudes we have absorbed in the past. There is so much more. Jesus came to recruit friends and

lovers. He didn't come to make us religious, wise, faithful, or even generous. Certainly, these can all be amazing
qualities, but if they don't flow from the heart of a lover,
it's not a true fit (1 Corinthians 13:1–13).

There's a question that regularly rings in my head.
After Jesus's death and resurrection, he had a heart-
to-heart with his friend Peter. Peter was so fearful the
night Jesus was arrested that he completely denied
even knowing Jesus. Not once, but *three* times. Can
you imagine how deeply that betrayal hurt Jesus and
how much shame it brought to Peter? Peter abandoned his closest friend in his greatest time of need.
When Jesus came back to life and next spoke to Peter,
he asked only one thing: "Do you love me?" (John
21:15–17). He didn't ask, "Do you believe in me?"
That answer was definitely settled by the resurrection.
Peter had watched Jesus die and now saw him alive
again. Jesus asked, "Do you love me?" Three times
Jesus questioned Peter. The first two times Jesus used
the word *agape* for love (remember this means faithful, selfless, and sacrificial). The third time Jesus used
the word *phileo* for love, which is rooted in friendship and brotherly affection. Jesus was asking Peter,
"Do you really love me and are you my friend?" Peter
needed to have the answer seared into his heart and
mind. So do we.

I remember a specific time when I was on the phone with a very close friend of mine named Rick. He is a great guy—an excellent athlete, successful entrepreneur, faithful husband, father, and friend. He even wears jeans sometimes. For many years he had been reading the Bible daily, growing in his faith and seeking to live a faithful life. All of this is awesome, but I remember the day Rick called and said something had changed. This day, he knew that God wanted his heart. He realized that going to church, praying, and helping others wasn't about a checklist to get God to love him more. He said, "Rob, I just realized something. I just realized that I love God. I go to church now because I want to worship him, not because I feel guilty if I don't go. When I read the Bible, it's not because I think it's something that I have to do. It's now because it's something that I want to do. I just realized that when I give my money or time to help others, it's not to attract people to me or so that God will see what I'm doing and be impressed. It's because I really love him and really care for others. Rob," he said, "I love God!"

Wow! That's where I want to be. That's the sweet spot: a place of fit and comfort where we all need to hang out. Love is the beginning and the end of all that God wants. Jesus didn't come for our belief; he came for our hearts. He is looking for friends and lovers.

··············· **REFLECTION** ·················

I believe Jesus goes eye-to-eye and heart-to-heart with you and me and asks us the same questions he asked Peter: "Do you love me? Do you *really* love me? Are you my friend?" This is an opportunity for us to take a few moments and quiet our hearts before God. Let's ask him to speak, and let's listen for his whisper to our souls. We need to be honest, because he knows our hearts. Are we willing to ask God to change our hearts and make us passionate friends and lovers so that all we do flows out of that love? Are we ready to put on that pair of jeans?

Two

...

LOVING YOURSELF

I spend much of my time meeting with people over coffee, pizza, or some kind of athletic activity. It's a joy for me to just hang out and speak with old friends and new friends (and even strangers). I listen a lot and really enjoy getting to know people and coming alongside them as a friend. Somewhere in the conversation (between sips and bites or deep breaths from exercise) I usually ask this short but penetrating question: "How is your heart?" The question often startles people (unless they have met with me before), but I am surprised by how many are willing to open up with a response that goes beyond the superficial.

Over the years as a friend, mentor, counselor, and pastor, I have come to see that while we tend to think about ourselves a lot, very few of us really like or love ourselves in a healthy way. That may sound funny in a culture that is often all about "me," but I do think it's accurate. We tend to have our thoughts and self-identity shaped early in life by how others treat us and what others say about us—and very often it isn't constructive.

Jesus taught much about loving our neighbors, but he linked it to how we love ourselves. Jesus didn't say, "Love your neighbor *instead of* or *more than* yourself." He said, "Love your neighbor *as* yourself" (Matthew 22:39). So I think it is important to consider what it means to love ourselves in a way that is healthy and not selfish or self-destructive. Jesus takes it as a given that we will love ourselves. However, he sets the context for what that love is to look like if it's going to be healthy and even holy.

It is my deep conviction that God's love within us is what enables us to really love ourselves and others in a healthy way. Self-love seeks to minimize pain and maximize comfort and happiness. This is fine in and of itself, but if it is not immersed in God's love, flowing through us and into others, it will be selfish, damaging, and potentially dangerous. This is why Jesus wedded our love for others and our love for ourselves together.

Life-giving love begins when the flow of God's love saturates our own hearts. Once we are saturated, God's love can flow through us to others. When love flows that way, it's healthy and real and breeds life.

In Leviticus 19 (that's where Jesus quoted the command "Love your neighbor as you love yourself" from), God gave Moses a list of instructions to pass on to the community. The list is prefaced with this: "You must be holy because I . . . am holy" (Leviticus 19:2). This word "holy" means many things. It is a Hebrew word that means to be set apart and dedicated to God: pure, innocent, free from impurity. God is saying to us, "Listen, I'm unique. I'm different. I'm the one and only God. If you are going to be my child, then you must be different also. You won't live like everyone else lives. You can't, because you belong to me. You won't think like everyone else thinks. You can't, because you belong to me. You won't speak like everyone else does, because you belong to me! You are to be holy, set apart, distinct—because that's who I am!" This doesn't mean that we have to be weird, strange, or obnoxious (although that comes naturally for many of us); it means that things change when we walk with God. Our lives will stand out because people will sense true and sincere love in our words and actions—the kind of love that can only come from God.

All of the instructions we find in the scripture here are

ultimately based upon who God is. There's a phrase that keeps being repeated. God keeps saying it's important to do this and do that because "I am the Lord." If you are a parent, maybe you can relate to this. Once in a while I find myself saying something similar to this to my kids. Sometimes when I ask them to do something, their first response is to ask, "Why?" (Don't you love that question?) I may take time to explain and help them understand what has led me to this request, but that doesn't always bring them on board. Other times, I may not feel it's necessary to explain why, for instance, they need to actually clean their room (so in case of emergency someone could actually find them). So sometimes I simply say, "Because I'm your dad and I asked you to." God says that sometimes too. It's important that we remember, though, that when it comes to God's instructions and requests for us, the context is always love.

Yes, here's the key that is so crucial for us to comprehend, because it is foundational to everything else. We've already discussed it, but let me repeat it: we are loved by God. Most of us say we get this, but we really don't. Jesus was so serious (deadly serious) about this that he gave his life so that we could know that God loves us! God wants you and me to know his love, to be able to receive his love, and to respond to his love. Only in doing that can our hearts be healed. And only in doing that can we—in a right and healthy way—love ourselves and love our neighbors. It begins with finally being able to admit, to acknowledge, and to receive the abundant love of God.

Why is it so hard for us to really believe in and accept and feel the love of God? For one thing, through the years and especially as children, most of us received a lot of bad teaching about God. And ultimately, we just live in a broken world. According to the Bible, there's been a battle raging in the cosmos since long before you and I showed up on the scene. Our souls have an enemy seeking to bring devastation and destruction. Scripture calls the enemy many names, like Satan, the devil, the dragon, the deceiver, the liar, the murderer, the thief. Many argue about the existence of evil. For me, it just takes a glance at the daily headlines or an overview of history. Some prefer to understand evil as primarily a result of bad, misguided, or illogical choices. I think it goes much deeper than that. The Bible simply makes it clear that evil is personified in a being as well as generalized in cultures, nations, and social systems. There's been a battle raging, and at birth we entered into a war zone here on planet Earth—a war for our very souls.

So our hearts are already tainted coming into the world and they start getting more broken from day one. Do you know why? Because our parents, as loving as they are or were (or weren't), were also wounded and broken. They were hurting and they passed some of that on to us, and then we became more broken because of some of our own choices—as well as the choices of others. We responded in ways that we shouldn't have, and there have been consequences. We need to admit that we're wounded. And when we do, we can begin to grasp the amazing truth that Jesus Christ came in love to forgive us and to heal us.

Remember that prophet—Isaiah? He described what Jesus, the Messiah, would do for us when he wrote, "He was pierced for our rebellion, crushed for our sins. He was beaten so we could be whole. He was whipped so we could be healed. . . . The Lord laid on him the sins of us all" (Isaiah 53:5–6).

The sad thing is that our default setting generally is to think about what we want and what we need or think we need. Our culture seems determined to keep us shallow and superficial—focused on our appearance, our clothing, what we drive, and where we live. Life can be all about what we own and what other people think about us. And so self-love easily becomes perverted and distorted. Instead of sacrificial and life-giving love, our appetites become addictive. We often turn to drugs, self-destructive behavior, and whatever feels good because this self-love has been distorted. It's been broken away from the love of God and from our love for others.

If we are not living in the flow of loving God and loving others, then our self-love quickly becomes unhealthy, selfish, and destructive.

It's not wrong for us to want to minimize pain and to maximize comfort and joy. It's just that we need to want the same for others—equally—and that's unnatural. Our heart of hearts bends toward "I want you to be happy; I just want to be happier. I want you to be blessed; I just want to be more blessed! I want you to have nice things; I just want to have more nice things than you!" This is the human heart at its best apart from the love of God. We can want good for others; we just want better for ourselves.

As we consider loving our neighbor as we love ourselves, the things that we want for ourselves should also be what we want for others. The happiness, the blessings, the forgiveness, the salvation, the joyful life that we want for ourselves should also be what we want for others. This desire of good for others should then shape how we treat them. In Matthew 7:12, Jesus puts it this way: "Do to others whatever you would like them to do to you. This is the essence of all that is taught in the law and the prophets."

It's important for us to acknowledge that apart from the love of God, we will never love people to that depth. It's just not inside of us on our own. On our own, it's mostly about "me." Even self-destructive behavior is often about "me." The pain that we bring to other people's lives because of the choices we make is never a result of true love flowing through us. This is why Jesus came to cleanse, heal, and bring us new hearts.

Let's revisit the promise God made through the prophet Ezekiel:

> Then I will sprinkle clean water on you, and you will be clean. Your filth will be washed away, and you will no longer worship idols. And I will give you a new heart, and I will put a new spirit in you. I will take out your stony, stubborn heart, and give you a tender, responsive heart. And I will put my Spirit in you so that you will follow my decrees and be careful to obey my regulation. (Ezekiel 36:25–27)

With God's Spirit and this new heart within us, we can truly love him with our heart, soul, mind, and strength—all that we are—and love others as we love ourselves. Finally, we can want for our spouse everything that we desire for ourselves; for our children, everything that we hope for ourselves; for our parents and friends and even for those people with whom we don't get along and whom we've struggled to like—we can want for them what we want for ourselves. This is what it means to love others as we love ourselves. This is what Jesus is talking about. This is the flow of love that God desires: from him, in and through us, reaching out to others.

Several years ago, three friends and I pedaled bikes coast to coast from San Francisco to the Jersey shore. We did a meandering four-thousand-mile trip to raise funds for what is now called Pillar College. I remember riding into western Pennsylvania, into a town called Confluence. It's considered one of the great kayaking areas of our nation. The town is named Confluence because it's where several tributaries, streams, and rivers all come together. For kayakers, it's ideal because they can keep going from one tributary to another while hardly ever having to get out. Confluence is a place where all the streams converge and flow together.

This is what loving God and loving others as ourselves is all about: when we receive the amazing love of God and respond by loving God with all that we are, when we allow his love to flow through us so that we can love ourselves and—out of that— love others, everything comes together. That's the place of comfort where the jeans fit just right and are durable. That's the ideal flow of love here on planet Earth, and it all begins with God first loving us.

Let's look briefly at one guy who met Jesus and really came to understand this. We get to see the very moment that this "confluence" came together in his life. Zacchaeus was well known for being rich and short and not always on the up-and-up in his business dealings. Zac's heart was wounded and so he took his self-love that was separated from God and others and made it all about himself. His love became centered on money and wealth and power and control. The story goes like this: Jesus was on his way toward Jerusalem and walked through the town called Jericho, where Zac lived. Zac had a thriving and somewhat shady business there as a tax collector. He made the big bucks, but that didn't bring him real meaning or joy. He had heard about this amazing rabbi named Jesus who was full of wisdom and love and had the power of God, the power to heal and perform miracles. Zac desperately wanted to meet Jesus or even just look at him, but he was so short he couldn't see over the crowd. So he did what any entrepreneur (or young boy) would do and climbed a tree to get high enough to see Jesus. Jesus actually walked right up to that tree and called Zac by name and demanded that he come down so that they could meet and spend some time together. Wow—what a moment, huh? This is where it all started coming together, and where Zac received his favorite pair of jeans. The Bible says,

Zacchaeus quickly climbed down and took Jesus to his house in great excitement and joy. But the people were displeased. "He has gone to be the guest of a notorious sinner," they grumbled. Meanwhile, Zacchaeus stood before the Lord and said, "I will give half my wealth to the poor, Lord, and if I have cheated people on their taxes, I will give them back four times as much!" Jesus responded, "Salvation has come to this home today, for this man has shown himself to be a true son of Abraham. For the Son of Man came to seek and save those who are lost." (Luke 19:1–10)

Zacchaeus was clearly blown away. He understood religious rules and rituals but had no clue how special he was and that God loved him. This man, who did not understand or live a life of love, was broken, hungry and thirsty at the deepest level of the soul. There he was, up in a tree (literally and figuratively), and I can imagine him wondering, "How does Jesus even know my name? I never met him before—but he called me by my name. Not only that—Jesus wants to spend time with me. I can't believe it! He wants to come to my house!" So Zac came down, and it says here that he received Jesus into his house with joy! Other people complained, saying,

"Look at Jesus—he's gone to be the guest of a sinner." But Zac wasn't complaining. For the first time in his life, love broke through. He knew that he was loved by God. He received this love that was brought to him that day in Jesus. And check this out—as God's love flowed through him, immediately his heart changed toward others. Zac stands up and announces, "I will give half my wealth to the poor." Imagine what a surprise that was to those who knew him and were listening! Half of everything! What if we did that today? Can we say, "Jesus, here and now, half of my wealth is going to help others because now I finally get it—you love me! I've been empty with the meaningless things that I've been trying to fill my soul with and now I am finally filled with your love. Lord, I've been awakened to a love that I've never known before—a love for others. This day, half of my wealth I give to the poor and if I have cheated anyone out of anything, I will pay them back four times!" Then, can you hear Jesus say to you, "Salvation has come to this home today, for this one has shown himself to be a true son (or daughter) of Abraham. For the Son of Man came to seek and save those who are lost."

Here's the beauty, my friend: you and I are often like Zacchaeus hanging out on that limb. Jesus stops, looks straight at us, and says, "Please come down from that tree. Come on! I know your name and I love you. I've been pursuing you—come on down! I don't care what others think. I want to spend time with you." Jesus is calling us by name today—specifically, saying "I love you, I've come for you. Now receive my love and let my love change you."

A few years ago, I was in Costa Rica visiting some of our mission churches there. One of the churches had a large tent next to a bar, and homeless addicts lived under a bridge nearby. Like Jesus, this church reaches out to addicts and feeds, loves, and cares for them. I was there one day when a man came who was about my age. I looked into his eyes. There, I could see all the pain, agony, guilt, shame, and self-hatred. In that moment, I caught a glimpse of the broken relationships, the broken hearts, and all the loneliness, addictions, and everything else that had crushed his soul. My friends began to pour love into him, and I began to see something change in his eyes as the love of God broke through. He began to weep as he believed for the first time that God loved him. As they gathered around him and the drugs were pulled from his pocket and put on the table, I could see something beautiful being born in his eyes. It was an amazing experience.

I imagine that's what it was like for Zacchaeus, and that's what it's like for you and me when we finally start to comprehend that we are deeply loved by God. In that healing love, we can finally love ourselves as we allow the love of Christ to flow into us and then through us into others. We can't love ourselves in any kind of healthy way until we embrace the love of God. Listen closely. Do you hear that? Someone is calling your name.

·················· **REFLECTION** ··················

Most of us know what it's like to be stuck up in a tree or hanging out on a limb. We know what took Zacchaeus there, but what has taken us there? And what will bring us down? Let's ask God to fill us with the kind of love that changed Zacchaeus. This is where we come to life. This is the confluence in which God's love flows. This is all that God has ever wanted or hoped for in us. It's time to embrace God's love. Don't be passive about that. Don't wait for lightning to strike. Jesus has already come. Jesus is looking right at us. He's calling our name. Are we listening? Are we ready to come down from the tree and welcome Jesus into our house?

Three

...

LOVING OTHERS

Hopefully we're beginning to understand that Jesus wants our lives with him to be real and natural so that our hearts become most comfortable when we're walking with him (like that great pair of broken-in jeans). Our hearts are most fully alive when we are caught up in this confluence of love that flows from him, in and through us, and out to others.

Remember, it all begins with love. Until or unless we get this right, nothing is right. Jesus essentially said, "Take everything that God requires, package it, roll it up, and squeeze it together." What do you come up with? It is this: to love him passionately and to love others as we love ourselves. It's all vitally connected (Matthew 22:36–40).

If we're going to love our neighbor, we need to know who our neighbor is. It definitely includes that nice couple across the street, but it also includes that not-so-nice guy a few houses over. But Jesus defines "neighbor" way beyond the boundaries of our neighborhood or apartment complex.

Jesus was in the midst of a Q&A session one day when an expert in religious law asked him what was needed to inherit eternal life. Jesus asked the lawyer if he knew what Moses had to say about it, and the man answered in words familiar to us now: "'You must love the Lord your God with all your heart, all your soul, all your strength, and all your mind.' And, 'Love your neighbor as yourself'" (Luke 10:27). Good answer, Jesus said, now go and do it.

The lawyer then followed up and asked Jesus who his neighbor was. So Jesus told him a story about a Jewish man who got brutally robbed and beaten while traveling from Jerusalem to Jericho (remember that's the town where Zac the tree climber met Jesus). He was essentially left for dead, but along came first a Jewish priest and second a Jewish temple assistant. Surely one of them would help this poor man. Right? Wrong! They both kept on walking, showing no love or mercy even though they were fellow Jews (and very religious ones at that). After this a Samaritan walked by. This is the guy everyone would have expected to keep walking, but what did he do? Jesus said,

> When he saw the man, he felt compassion for him. Going over to him, the Samaritan soothed his wounds with olive oil and wine and bandaged them. Then he put the man on his own donkey and took him to an inn, where he took care of him. The next day he handed the innkeeper two silver coins, telling him, "Take care of this man. If his bill runs higher than this, I'll pay you the next time I'm here." (Luke 10:33–35)

Now it was Jesus's turn to ask the question. He looked at the lawyer and asked, "Now which of these three would you say was a neighbor to the man who was attacked by bandits?" The lawyer responded, "The one who showed him mercy" (Luke 10:36–37). That's right, Jesus said, now go and be that man.

As usual, Jesus goes for the jugular and says some seriously radical stuff. Here's a little insight: In the first century, Jews mainly considered their neighbors to be other Jews. It was cultural. Greeks and Romans regarded a neighbor to be the one who was near to them. It was locational—similar to what most people in our culture today would define it as. Jesus makes it clear that God doesn't recognize those definitions. Everyone is our neighbor, whether they're our family, our enemy, our colleague at work, the homeless man downtown, or the orphan in India. Jesus came in the flesh to redefine what it means for us to love our neighbor. He lived it out and even died for his neighbors—past, present, and future. That includes us.

The unlikely hero of Jesus's story was a Samaritan. Samaritans were not well liked by the Jews in that day, and the feeling was mutual. If we rewrote this parable using contemporary language, it might include a Palestinian coming to the aid of a Jew, or a Protestant helping a Catholic in Northern Ireland, or a gang member helping someone injured from a rival gang. These kinds of interactions just don't usually happen. Jews didn't hang out with Samaritans in those days. In fact, they would travel out of their way to avoid going through Samaria, even if it added thirty or forty miles to their trip (by foot!).

Jesus was redefining "neighbor" by using an example of someone who the listening crowd didn't like very much—and Jesus took it a step further by establishing him as the hero of the story! The Samaritan's background and culture weren't important to Jesus. The Samaritan was the one pleasing God by the way he loved someone in need, and that's what truly mattered.

In Jesus's story, the devoutly religious guys showed up first and did the culturally acceptable (however unloving) act of walking right on by. That wouldn't seem strange to the audience—it was normal behavior. Then the Samaritan comes down the road and he sees this injured man and feels compassion for him. He did the culturally unexpected and unacceptable (but right and loving) thing. That would have been shocking to those listening. This is what Jesus is calling us to. This Samaritan's heart was genuine because he felt and showed compassion for this victim when no one else was around. There weren't any cameras or eyewitnesses. He wasn't going to receive the Nobel Peace Prize or get interviewed on prime-time television. He was alone and he saw this man and there wasn't anyone to impress, yet he still helped him.

This Samaritan hero of ours was willing to get messy, be inconvenienced, and act against what was expected or considered acceptable by his culture and peers. The man who was beaten and robbed was bloody, half dead, and a stranger. It's never enjoyable to reach into another person's mess. But God is asking us to do that. He asks us to care and be willing to get involved—and maybe even get dirty on behalf of others. And most often it will cost us something—certainly our convenience, our time, and maybe even our money. This is one of those times when the gospel and our blue jeans won't feel too comfortable to wear—at least not at first. This will stretch us. Our unlikely hero used his own time and resources to help this wounded stranger. He cleaned and bandaged his wounds and put him on his own donkey (right on the leather seat!) and took him to the inn himself. Then he paid for the man to be cared for until he was strong and healthy enough to get back on his own feet. Hopefully, we are getting the message here.

Sure, loving our neighbor may include loaning that cup of sugar to the sweet lady next door. But we also need to be willing to stop everything and make sacrifices on behalf of the stranger-neighbor who crosses our path. That's part of loving our neighbor as we love ourselves and treating others the way we want to be treated (Luke 6:31). Let's not be like those two religious guys who rationalized with a pious glance the other way. God doesn't mind, and even prefers, that we come to his table with hands messy from loving others.

REFLECTION

In the beginning of the story, Jesus said the Samaritan "felt compassion," and then, at the end of the story, Jesus said that he "showed him mercy." Then Jesus said, "Go and do the same."

This is a good time to consider who in our life needs our compassion, forgiveness, or mercy. Who might God be asking us to share our resources or time with, or otherwise get messy for, so that we can truly love our neighbors as ourselves? If we are going to walk with Jesus, these are the roads he will take us down as he asks us to be the good neighbor.

Part II

LIVING AS JESUS LIVED

Four

...

LIVING RELATIONALLY

I t's really easy to get distracted by things that aren't important, or even things that are important but not *most* important. Many things glitter but few are truly worth our time and passion. If we aren't careful, most of our days can fly by with us focused primarily on things that aren't primary. This leads to a heavily populated place of deep regrets that none of us want to find ourselves in. One night, in September of 1999, I was freshly awakened to this.

The tropical storm remnants of a hurricane named Floyd had caused some serious flooding in many coastal areas of the United States, including the part of New Jersey where my family and I live. Our college and church ministry campus was hammered by rain as the clouds seemed to lock themselves overhead. As the water rose and we began evacuations of residents there, I was deeply discouraged, thinking of the major damage to our facilities. I was also caught up in thoughts about all the mess and major work that was ahead in trying to rebuild and restore. Although my faith in God was strong, I wondered where he was, and what he was thinking.

In the midst of all the chaos, I got separated from and lost contact with my wife. I became fearful, and suddenly the buildings and offices, the furniture and supplies, and all the mess and loss didn't mean a thing. All I thought about, prayed for, and put my effort into was finding my wife and knowing that she was safe. The two hours of uncertainty were extremely emotional as I paddled about in a boat searching for her. When I finally found Debra—sitting and waiting on a rooftop—all was well with the world. All the realities of the flood and damage and loss were still very real, but it really didn't matter much anymore. I was reminded again that night (and many days and nights since then) about true priorities and that life is not about the stuff—even if that stuff is good. Life is really all about people—all about relationships.

If we really have a heart to walk closely with Jesus, then we need to be willing to have some of our passions and priorities change so that we can share in *his* passions and priorities. It may seem like a sacrifice at first, but soon it will become our sweet spot and comfort zone. That's just how loving relationships work. Jesus didn't hide his passions and priorities from us. As we read through the gospels, it becomes clear that wherever Jesus was, there were people, and wherever people were, there was Jesus. People were his priority. His mission and passion was to rescue and save the world (including you and me).

Jesus lived relationally. Everything for Jesus was about relationships—relationships with his Father, and relationships with others. Some of us are strong extroverts. We are energized by being with others, so living relationally sounds fairly easy. Others of us are strong introverts. Being around too many people for too long can be draining and stressful. If that's you, don't start groaning yet. Living relationally doesn't mean that we have to be in large groups all the time. But it does mean we will value relationships over assets and schedules and project lists. It does mean that friendships and the needs of others will become a greater priority in our lives. If we are going to walk with Jesus, we need to live relationally—no matter where we are on the extrovert-introvert scale.

For me, the extrovert, I can meet with people all day long, most every day, and really enjoy life. I may get worn out and need a break once in a while, but soon I'm ready to jump right back in. For my wife, the introvert, relationships are built with fewer people, but still very deeply. Whether we connect deeply with many or few in our lifetime, the good news is that Jesus focuses on quality over quantity and he simply asks us to be who we are, for him.

In the gospel of John, chapter 14, Jesus says if we love and obey him, then he and God the Father will come to us in a real and intimate way. Jesus also promised to send the Holy Spirit to us. Jesus was speaking about the relationship he had shared from eternity with the Father and with the Holy Spirit—this is the relationship he wants to share with us. That's a pretty wild thought.

When we read the gospels, the first thing we see Jesus do as he builds his core group is say, "Come, follow me"(Matthew 4:18–22). He was looking for those who were willing to spend time with him, walk with him, and be his friend. He wanted to have some close friends to pour his heart and life into and to share in the journey and mission with him. This remains the heart and hope of the Lord Jesus today. He is still looking for and pursuing people who will follow him and be his true friends.

I know this idea may sound a little too "common" for the God of the universe, but it's important to realize that church isn't some building we simply go to for worship. The true church isn't an organization or a place; it is simply composed of all those who have taken Jesus up on his amazing invitation to know and follow him and be filled with his Spirit. Then, we come together as a family to worship and serve and grow closer to him and encourage one another.

It makes me smile when I think about the first miracle that Jesus performed, in a place called Cana of Galilee. It's recorded in John, chapter 2. Jesus and his closest friends (disciples) attended a wedding, and there he changed gallons and gallons of water into fine wine. What kind of opening miracle is that? Shouldn't the Messiah, who came to save the world, have a higher priority and more significant way to launch his ministry? But in this case Jesus was hanging out with his buddies at a wedding for a young Hebrew couple. Jewish weddings were long and filled with celebration, singing, dancing, and—yes—wine.

In that day and culture, running out of wine was a major social blunder that would bring great embarrassment to the family. Mary (Jesus's mom) was there and came up to ask her boy to do something to help them out. She cared about this young couple and wanted to lend a hand. She knew that her son wasn't just special (as every mom believes); she knew he was also the Son of God. Jesus essentially said, "Not now, Mom—it's not my time yet." But Mary was persistent (like many of our moms) and Jesus agreed. He prayed to the Father and turned gallons of water into the finest wine. Isn't that amazing? The Savior of the world took time to listen to his mom and then keep a young couple from social embarrassment. He did that because relationships (including yours and mine) are a priority to Jesus. He is a relational Savior.

I also think about the children. In Jesus's time and culture, children were not the priority of the day. The disciples tried to keep the kids away because they thought Jesus was a rabbi who was too important and busy for their childish noise and energy. While they were all pushing to keep the kids away, Jesus had his own idea: "Let the children come to me. Don't stop them! For the Kingdom of Heaven belongs to those who are like these children" (Matthew 19:14). Then we read that Jesus took the children into his arms and blessed them. Wouldn't you have loved to be one of those children? I'm sure they never forgot that moment.

Throughout scripture, Jesus shows us—like the story of the Samaritan hero we discussed in chapter 3—that he's willing to get messy, be inconvenienced, and act against what is expected or considered acceptable by the current culture on behalf of people—on behalf of us—because relationships matter. People matter.

When I think about Jesus living a relational life, I also think about the woman at the well. Maybe you remember her story? She was a community outcast known for five failed marriages and was now living with a man who wasn't her husband. Nobody had time for her. Nobody wanted to be seen in public with her. When this woman came to the well for water, she came alone during the heat of the day when no one else would be there. No one wanted to socialize with her—except maybe the men, but that was only behind closed doors for their own pleasure. Nobody truly cared or wanted to speak to her. Nobody, that is, except Jesus.

Jesus stood by that well with her and had the audacity to ask her for a drink. She was shocked! Jesus was not just a man, but a Jew, and he was speaking to her in public—which was against the social code of the day. To make it worse, this woman was—of all things—a Samaritan (like our Samaritan friend from chapter 3)! Once again, Jesus shows he has his own standards, and they aren't influenced by cultural biases.

Jesus went on to tell this woman that it was really she who needed a drink, not he. He offered her "living water" and the promise to never thirst again. This broken and unloved woman came to see that this wasn't just another empty promise from just another man who wanted to take advantage of her. She heard real love in his words, in the tone of his voice, and in the way he looked at her. She also sensed Jesus's true authority and power and became convinced that he was the Messiah. Why did Jesus take time for this woman when no one else would? Because she was precious to him; because he's a relational Savior; and because she was (and we are) his mission. (For the full story, read John 4:1–42.)

When I think about Jesus living relationally, I think about the name that the very religious people called him in mockery. They got so upset and frustrated with Jesus for not fitting into their mold of a respected rabbi. They tried to come up with an offensive name to call him, and the best they could come up with was "friend of sinners" (Matthew 11:19; Luke 7:34). Instead of this bothering Jesus, he embraced that title. Jesus told them he came so those who were broken could find hope and life again. He came so those who were lost could be found (Luke 9:10). So yes, he was (and is) a friend of sinners—absolutely!

They also called Jesus a drunk and a glutton because he went to parties. That didn't bother Jesus either. He went wherever he could find people hungry for truth, in need of hope and healing, in search of a Savior in their heart of hearts (Matthew 9:12–13). Jesus didn't get all dressed up and wait in the temple until people got their act together and came to him. Jesus took the blue jeans gospel to the streets and pursued the hearts of the lost and broken.

One of the stories that moves me most deeply is something recorded in chapter 11 of the gospel of John. Here's the setting: Jesus had dear friends. Mary, Martha, and Lazarus—two sisters and a brother. While Jesus and his disciples were away on a journey, his friend Lazarus became sick and died. Four days later, Jesus and the disciples arrived to the home of these dear friends. The first one Jesus ran into was Martha, and she said, "Lord, if only you had been here, my brother would not have died. But even now I know that God will give you whatever you ask" (John 11:21–22). When Jesus then told Martha that Lazarus was going to come back to life, she said that she knew he would, on the last day when everyone would rise again. Then Jesus responded, "I am the resurrection and the life. Anyone who believes in me will live, even after dying. Everyone who lives in me and believes in me will never ever die" (John 11:25–26). When Jesus asked Martha if she believed this, she said yes and then went and got her sister. When Mary got up to go see Jesus, all the friends and neighbors who were mourning with her followed her to make sure she was okay. When Jesus saw Mary and all the others weeping with her, he became deeply emotional and even very angry. He wasn't angry at them—he was angry at death and the pain and suffering that had never been part of God's plan. Together they went toward the cave where Lazarus's body had been laid, and in the midst of the journey, the Bible simply says, "Jesus wept." (For the full story, read John 11:21–44.)

Jesus wept. This wasn't just a couple of tears and a few sniffles. This literally means he broke down uncontrollably. He totally lost it emotionally because he saw the sorrow and felt the pain and loss that humanity feels. He felt it all; it was so real to him. It wasn't just for Lazarus, Mary, and Martha. I believe he wept that day for you and me as well. He wept for what was lost as a result of our rebellion and choices. He wept for the brokenness that comes to us in this world as a result of its arrogance and selfishness. He wept because of the pain and the unnatural death that we suffer that were not originally God's intent. He wept that day because he's the relational Savior who loves and cares deeply.

But Lazarus's story doesn't end there. In the midst of his anger and weeping, Jesus arrived at the tomb and told the people there to roll the stone away from the entrance. But Martha (like a good sister) was very concerned about what they would see and smell if the tomb were opened.

Instead of listening to Martha's concerns,

> Jesus responded, "Didn't I tell you that you would see God's glory if you believe?" So they rolled the stone aside. Then Jesus looked up to

heaven and said, "Father, thank you for hearing me. You always hear me, but I said it out loud for the sake of all these people standing here, so they will believe that you sent me." Then Jesus shouted, "Lazarus, come out!" And the dead man came out, his hands and feet bound in graveclothes, his face wrapped in a headcloth. Jesus told them, "Unwrap him and let him go!" (John 11:40–44)

Wow—what a crazy moment. Lazarus had been clearly dead and decomposing in the heat for four days. He was wrapped up in linen strips like a mummy. Jesus told them to take off Lazarus's graveclothes because they were the wrappings of a dead man. Lazarus was alive! Jesus had just told Martha, "I am the resurrection and the life. Anyone who believes in me will live, even after dying. Everyone who lives in me and believes in me will never ever die." Yes, we will all physically die. Lazarus did eventually die again years later. But ultimate death—the death of the soul—will never be able to touch those who believe. How amazing it must have felt for Lazarus to be unbound by those graveclothes and to put on his favorite pair of jeans (or robe) again!

The list goes on and on and on. Everywhere Jesus went we find him stopping, listening, speaking, caring, and touching. He spent time with lepers and liars, soldiers, thieves, politicians, intellectuals, rich, poor, prostitutes, and anyone else who cried out to him. Right before Jesus's last breath, when he was dying on the cross—when his blood was already pouring out for our forgiveness—he was bringing salvation to a dying thief hanging next to him (Luke 23:39–43). In the midst of incredible torture, he still managed to show concern and make plans for the care of his mother after his death (John 19:25–27).

There's really only one reason that I can write this book. It's because Jesus is a friend of sinners, and he has pursued a relationship with me. Jesus came for me and he's my Lord and Savior and friend. Jesus came for you, too. He came for us because he's the relational Savior— because we are his passion and mission.

If we're going to truly follow Jesus, relationships need to become our priority, because relationships are *his* priority. This will change things. It means that blind beggar guy is someone we can't just walk past anymore, because Jesus stops there to listen and help. It means when we see that drug addict or person being exploited on the street, we can't just walk past and judge anymore; we need to look for a way to offer them life and healing in Jesus, because Jesus is already there. It means that we will keep our promises and honor our covenants. We can't abandon our marriages anymore, because God takes this covenant very seriously—and for those of us who are married, our marriages must be a priority. It means that if we have children, our children are our priority—above our jobs or bank accounts or hobbies. It means if we have parents, we don't forget about them. We don't walk away from them; we are faithful to them. It's time we reach out to people in need and help them and make the people in our lives our passion and mission. This is part of what the blue jeans gospel is all about.

·············· **REFLECTION** ··············

Like he did for that woman at the well, Jesus offers you and me a drink of living water, also. And like he did to Lazarus, he calls us out of the grave, too. Jesus is merciful and loving, and he may be standing at the cave entrance right now and telling us to get up, come out, and follow him. Jesus alone is the resurrection and the life and it's time to stop looking in other places. He wants us to be fully alive with him, to get out of those nasty graveclothes and into some jeans and walk with him. Have we said yes? Are we ready to change clothes? What priorities need to change in our lives if we are to walk with Jesus? Where do we need to get refocused? What relationships do we need to pour more into?

Five

...

LIVING WITH DAD

One of the things people noticed early on about Jesus was the difference in how he prayed and spoke about God. It seemed so much more real and friendly—even intimate—than anything they had ever heard before. Jesus presented the heart of God as the heart of someone who really cared and loved, and when Jesus prayed, he called God "Father." That was radical in those days. And even more radical, Jesus said that others could know God as their Father also.

Most of the people who were hanging out with Jesus in those early days were Jewish like him. They had heard and known about the one, true, living God ever since their birth. They had even been raised to recognize God as the Father of Israel. But that was still very different from being able to know and refer to God as a personal Father. That was way too close for comfort, and many felt like it was arrogant, dishonoring, and even blasphemous.

But still, people watched Jesus as he walked in gentleness and mercy. Far from being detached and arrogant, Jesus took time for the people who were poor, sick, and marginalized—people whom none of the other religious leaders seemed to have any time for. And through Jesus, some amazing things were happening. Blind people were seeing again, crippled people were walking, and others who were thought to be deeply mentally unstable or were under the control of evil spirits were restored to their right mind and seemed happy and at peace. So people continued to watch and listen as Jesus spoke about his relationship with God, his Father.

Another thing that these Jews were very familiar with was prayer. They prayed every day, even multiple times each day. Many of their prayers were connected to the ancient prayers of Israel and things that were found in the Hebrew scriptures. Other prayers had been memorized from the teachings of other rabbis. They were people of prayer, but watching and listening to Jesus pray was very different. His prayers were passionate. He prayed as though he really had a relationship with God and as though God knew him well. He prayed like he knew God was listening and responding. And when Jesus prayed, he called God "Father." There it was again. And some of the followers began to believe that it was true, that God really did love them as a Father and that through Jesus, they could know him that way too.

Some of us have had fathers who were loving, kind, and faithful. I had a dad like that. He was awesome! Because of that, the thought of knowing and calling God my Father is a pleasant one. But others of us have had a very different experience with our fathers and carry some deep wounds and heartache from that relationship. The thought of knowing God as or calling God "Father" may not be so positive or appealing. It's so important to see and understand that God is different. His fatherhood is not defined by how your earthly father treated you.

A few years after Jesus's death and resurrection, there was a young rabbi named Saul who was becoming well known. Saul had never met Jesus, but he hated him. He hated that Jesus had claimed to be the Messiah and was convinced Jesus was a liar. Saul also hated that some Jews were following Jesus and claiming that he rose again after he was crucified. As a young rabbi, Saul stood by while others stoned a Jewish follower of Jesus named Stephen. They killed him. They excused themselves for doing this, claiming that Stephen was guilty of blaspheming against God by calling Jesus the Messiah. In that time, even as it is today in some religions, blasphemy was considered worthy of the death penalty.

After this, Saul was hungry for more. He believed his anger and his actions were righteous and started traveling around the region to towns and synagogues, beating up Jewish followers of Jesus and having them arrested.

During one of his expeditions, Saul was literally knocked off his horse. He heard a loud voice and someone speaking to him. When he asked who it was, the response was, "I am Jesus, the one you are persecuting! Now get up and go into the city, and you will be told what you must do" (Acts 9:5–6). Saul was left blind. He was led into Damascus, and for three anxious days he had plenty of time to consider all the scriptures about the Messiah and all that he had experienced and heard. Somewhere in the midst of those anxious moments, Saul had a breakthrough. A Jewish follower of Jesus named Simon came and spoke and prayed with him, and his sight was restored. But much more than Saul's eyesight was restored. This man, who once hated Jesus and did violence to those who followed him, became a great friend and passionate follower of Jesus. His expeditions, from this point forward, were to tell others about Jesus, often risking (and ultimately giving) his life to do it. (Read more in the book of Acts, starting with chapter 8.)

A friend recently shared his observation with me that most of us, even followers of Jesus, live like we're orphans. We may have asked Jesus to forgive our sins and received him as our Savior, but we still live as if we don't have a Father—one who really knows and loves us and is always with us. So we may be faithful but completely miss out on the intimate relationship that is available with God, as well as the hope that is ours when we know we are a child dearly loved. We really are the apple of our Father's eye, but most of us don't live in that reality.

That's definitely not the reality Saul had been living in. He was a passionate and religious man, faithful to the letter of the Hebrew law and, he thought, to God. But when Saul (who from then on was called Paul) bowed his heart to Jesus as his Savior and Messiah, he also came to know God as his Father. Paul wrote many letters, which now comprise over half of what we call the New Testament. One of these letters was directed to Jewish and Gentile Christians in Rome. He wrote:

> So you have not received a spirit that makes you fearful slaves. Instead, you received God's Spirit when he adopted you as his own children. Now we call him, "Abba, Father." For his

Spirit joins with our spirit to affirm that we are
God's children. And since we are his children,
we are his heirs. In fact, together with Christ
we are heirs of God's glory. (Romans 8:15–17)

Paul wrote a similar thing to other followers of Jesus
in a city called Galatia:

But when the right time came, God sent his
Son, born of a woman, subject to the law. God
sent him to buy freedom for us who were slaves
to the law, so that he could adopt us as his very
own children. And because we are his children, God has sent the Spirit of his Son into
our hearts, prompting us to call out, "Abba,
Father." Now you are no longer a slave but
God's own child. And since you are his child,
God has made you his heir. (Galatians 4:4–7)

In both of these letters, Paul uses the term *abba*.
This is an Aramaic word that really has no direct English
translation, but it is a very affectionate and intimate
word reserved for a child and father—maybe closest to
the English word "daddy." It's pretty amazing that this
term "Abba, Father" was used by the once-prideful,

Jesus-hating rabbi who became the humble, passionate, and faithful Jesus-*loving* rabbi. Through Jesus, Paul
found the sweet spot and comfort zone of coming to
know God as his dear Father (Abba). He understood and
embraced the blue jeans gospel, and he wanted to make
sure that you and I know that this is our privilege and
need as well.

The relationship between Jesus and his Father is
so close and loving that he always wanted to make his
Father proud. He lived to honor the Father. Everything
was about this, and as we begin to walk closely with
Jesus, this will become our desire and passion, also.

We've gotten a close glimpse of Jesus, but what does
the Father look like? And what does it mean to honor
the Father? Even the closest friends and followers
(disciples)—who knew and walked with Jesus—carried
that question. So one day, as Jesus was preparing to lay
his life down for us and return to the Father, he had
this conversation with his close friends:

> "I am the way, the truth, and the life. No one
> can come to the Father except through me. If
> you had really known me, you would know
> who my Father is. From now on, you do know
> him and have seen him!"

Philip said, "Lord, show us the Father, and we will be satisfied."

Jesus replied, "Have I been with you all this time, Philip, and yet you still don't know who I am? Anyone who has seen me has seen the Father!" (John 14:6–9)

Jesus makes it clear that we don't have to look any further than to him to get a glimpse of the Almighty God and Everlasting Father. He said, "When you see me, you see the Father." When we look at Jesus, we see the very character, heart, and glory of the Father.

It's time we stop living as orphans and embrace that, through Jesus, God has become (or wants to become) our Father. Through this Father-child relationship, we come to really know who we are and find that sweet spot for our soul. We are *his* kids. We can live this life with identity and purpose. We are children of the King, Almighty God, Everlasting Father—that's great news, and it's the heart of the gospel.

In 1944, a couple by the name of Wilbur and Elsie Konkel were serving as missionaries in England. World War II was raging; these were dark and uncertain times, but this couple knew who they were. They knew their identities as followers of Jesus and children of the Father. They knew their purpose was to help people and share the love of Jesus, and they were known for how they loved God and cared for others.

The government gave these missionaries rations of orange juice and cod liver oil. The neighborhood children would come by and the couple made sure all of them received these precious supplies. The Konkels also formed children's Bible clubs and extended the love of Jesus to these kids.

Not far away, there was a single mother named Constance, who had three daughters. She had been abandoned by her husband and was overwhelmed. She couldn't physically care for her daughters any longer and they often roamed the streets seeking food to eat. This desperate mother reached out to the Konkels, who she knew loved God and loved children. With their agreement, Constance brought her three daughters on Christmas morning. Wilbur and Elsie, who had no children of their own, took these girls into their heart and home and became like parents to them. Later, they brought yet another young girl into their hearts and home.

Scripture tells us that Jesus took children into his arms and said, "Anyone who welcomes a little child like this on my behalf welcomes me, and anyone who welcomes me also welcomes my Father who sent me" (Luke 9:48). That's what the Konkels did. They welcomed Jesus when they took those three girls in on that Christmas morning in 1944. They didn't only welcome Jesus—they welcomed the Father, too. And you know their Father was proud of them.

The eldest of those little girls eventually grew up and became my mom. She was the big sister, but just a scared little nine-year-old child then. Because these followers of Jesus knew who they were as children of God, they knew their identity and purpose in life. They took these scared little girls and loved them. They made sacrifices and were willing to make the hard choices that changed the lives of these little ones forever. And, of course, that changed my life forever, too.

················ **REFLECTION** ················

Things changed radically when Saul (Paul) recog-
nized and received Jesus as Messiah and Savior.
In that moment he also entered into a relationship with God as his Abba, Father. This change
moved Paul beyond religion to being a son and
faithful follower. That experience and change is
available and crucial for all of us. Has that change
occurred within our hearts yet? Whether our
earthly father was exceptionally wonderful or
pretty much nonexistent, our Father God wants
us to know him as our loving and faithful Daddy
(Abba). Once Paul understood this truth and
how deeply loved he was, he began to live a new
life to please the Father. In what ways did Jesus
demonstrate his love for the Father? In what
ways did Paul? How should this love be demonstrated in our lives today?

Six

...

LIVING WITH
FORGIVENESS

Jesus tended to walk places that other people wouldn't walk. So—here on earth, following Jesus will definitely take us along paths that are less traveled. Jesus described the route as a "narrow gate" and a "difficult" path that few find (Matthew 7:13–14). We'll definitely want to be wearing a pair of comfortable and durable jeans for this journey. If we want to keep walking with Jesus, we will inevitably encounter junctions along the way where a choice must be made.

The great Hall of Fame baseball player Yogi Berra is reported to once have said, "When you come to a fork in the road—take it." Good advice. One of the many forks in the road that will affect everything is whether or not we will choose to live a life of forgiveness and peace or a life of condemnation and bitterness. This is one of those choices we must make on an almost daily basis as we live in relationship with other human beings.

Jesus taught and lived a life of forgiveness. I'm very grateful for that, because I certainly need a large amount of it! Forgiveness is core to Jesus's heart and life—it's essentially why Jesus put skin on and came to planet Earth.

People were deeply impacted by the way Jesus prayed, and one day those who were with Jesus asked him to teach them how to pray like he did. Jesus began by calling God "Father." We've already talked about how radical that was. Most of us have heard or even memorized the prayer often referred to as "the Lord's Prayer." Toward the end of the prayer it states, "Forgive us our sins, as we forgive those who sin against us." And then right after the prayer ends, Jesus says, "If you forgive those who sin against you, your heavenly Father will forgive you. But if you refuse to forgive others, your Father will not forgive your sins" (Matthew 6:12–15).

This critical element—forgiveness—becomes part of the road less traveled and makes all the difference. We cannot receive the deep forgiveness of God and live in that forgiveness if we are not willing to forgive others. This truth is like one of those huge vitamin pills in the morning that at times isn't easy to swallow but is really good for us. Forgiveness is core to the gospel of Jesus Christ. At times it will not be a very comfortable pair of jeans to put on, but once the jeans are broken in, they will fit well, feel great, and be extremely durable.

Once when Jesus tried to help people understand how compassionate and forgiving God is, he told a story of a father who had two sons. His younger son was proud, impatient, and rebellious. This son deeply hurt and disrespected his father and then abandoned the family. He took his portion of the family's estate, ran off, and completely wasted it in wild and destructive ways. When this selfish, rebellious, and unfaithful son was broke, hungry, and desperate, he began thinking about home. He decided to return and ask his father to allow him to be a servant in the home, because he knew he was not worthy to be a son.

What was the father's response? Certainly, he had every reason to reject the son outright, or at the very least severely discipline him. But the father watched, day after day, for the return of his wayward son. And, when he finally saw him in the distance, he *ran* to him! In that culture, a father's position was greatly respected and a respectable person didn't run to anyone. But this father hiked up his robe and shamelessly sprinted, filled with love and compassion. The father embraced and kissed his son and even threw a big welcome-home party. Now that's forgiveness. And that's a picture of how God forgives us. (Read the story in Luke 15:11–32.)

Jesus told this story to help us understand that when God forgives us, he isn't hesitant or halfhearted. God doesn't require us to beg and he doesn't hold our sin against us. Instead, Jesus shows that God is like the father whose son totally disrespected, dishonored, and abandoned him; when the son came back with very little hope and expectation—when he simply turned and began the journey home to the father—the father was watching and waiting to run to him! He was anxious to embrace and forgive! He was eager to say, "Welcome home!"

This father replaced the tattered clothes and dressed his son in the best robe in the house. He put sandals on his blistered feet and fully restored him to the family. Then he held an extravagant feast and proclaimed, "This son of mine was dead and has now returned to life. He was lost, but now he is found" (Luke 15:24). It's almost too good to be true, but Jesus says this is the heart of God, our Father. This is how he embraces us when our hearts move toward him in humility and sincerity.

David is considered to be the greatest king of Israel. He is also known for some really bad decisions that made a terrible mess of things. He understood what it was like to feel guilt and shame and to be deserving of God's judgment. He also came to know and experience, first-hand, the great mercy of God. As the prominent writer of Psalms, David reminds us how greatly blessed—how overwhelmingly fortunate and happy—is anyone whose sins have been forgiven by God. David goes on to say, "When I refused to confess my sin, my body wasted away, and I groaned all day long. . . . Finally, I confessed all my sins to you and stopped trying to hide my guilt. . . . And you forgave me! All my guilt is gone" (Psalm 32:3, 5).

Most of us, in our honest moments, recognize that we have often blown it. We've done some wrong and hurtful things. If the Lord treated us as we deserved, it wouldn't be a pretty picture. In another Psalm, David proclaims the good news that the Lord does not treat us as our sins deserve. Instead, we are told that "The Lord is like a father to his children, tender and compassionate. . . . He knows how weak we are" (Psalm 103:13–14). Our Father God is extravagant with his love, mercy, patience, and forgiveness. I hope we can truly embrace this concept: God is beautifully merciful and forgiving when we simply and sincerely turn our hearts toward him.

Further along this narrow path with Jesus, we are faced with the choice of extending this same type of forgiveness toward others. We are asked to also be extravagant in our mercy to those who have wronged us. Well, that's a whole other matter, isn't it? We all are eager to be so amazingly forgiven, but how painfully difficult it is to give this kind of mercy to others.

It's important to understand that forgiveness does not mean that the wrong committed against us is okay. Forgiveness does not mean that people are no longer responsible for their actions or that they should not—or will not—be held accountable for the wrong they have done. Forgiveness also does not mean that people will not face the consequences of their choices at some point, regardless of whether they are repentant. And, finally, forgiveness does not just mean that we look the other way and pretend it has not happened. Sin (disobedience to God's will and ways)—whether it's rebellion, arrogance, selfishness, lust, dishonesty, violence, neglect, or whatever—is a very serious offense. God does not take it lightly and we can't either.

The truth is that sin destroys, and God does not look the other way. Instead, God chose to come to us and pay the penalty for us. Jesus was whipped, beaten, tortured, bloodied, and murdered on the cross for all that we've done so that we could be forgiven. A heavy price was paid for our souls.

Jesus didn't come to earth and tell us that all our offenses are no longer serious. He didn't say, "No big deal, it's okay. Just forget about it." The gospel message is that we are guilty and deserving of death, but Jesus gave his own life for us instead.

Here are a few things that forgiveness *does* mean: Forgiveness does mean we release our own offenses—as well as our offenders—to God. It means we release our own guilt and the guilt of others to God. And we refuse to be handcuffed or controlled by shame or bitterness any longer. Forgiveness does mean that we will not seek revenge on the ones who have brought heartache to us—whether those people are ourselves or others. Forgiveness means we choose against our "right" to be the victim. Forgiveness means that we pray for our enemies (Matthew 5:44) and desire that they find the forgiveness, healing, and salvation of God. In the act of forgiving, we also release the forgiveness, healing, and blessing of the Father upon our own lives. Ultimately, it's coming full-face with the reality that we have been forgiven much—and the price was so great, how can we not forgive others?

Theologian and ethicist Lewis Smedes wrote, "Forgiveness is setting a prisoner free and discovering that the prisoner was you." So true! Unforgiveness imprisons and destroys us in our deepest self. That's most certainly one of the reasons God takes it so seriously. He knows what it does to the heart and soul of the human being. Jesus died so we could not just experience forgiveness, but freely distribute it as well.

Every person has been offended, hurt, and wounded. Some of us have suffered horrific evils by others. Many are being eaten up inside by bitter feelings and smoldering anger. But that acid of internal bitterness isn't just hurting the offender—it eats away at the one offended. Unforgiveness will emotionally chain us to the ones who have wronged us. Our thoughts are consumed by them. In fact, our bitterness works to harden our own hearts and often splashes onto innocent bystanders, even those we love.

You and I weren't forgiven because we deserved it. The people who betrayed Jesus and had him whipped and nailed to that tree didn't deserve his word from the bloodied cross: "Father, forgive them, for they don't know what they're doing." But he spoke it anyway.

Maybe the starting point for us is to acknowledge to the Lord that we just don't have it within us to forgive and that we need his help. God is able to make it possible for us to see our enemies from his perspective. Release that person to God, and God will be faithful to make things right. In fact, God's sense of justice is far better than our own—and for that, we can be thankful.

In Colossians 2:13–15, the apostle Paul tried to help people understand the significance of what Jesus has done for us. He wrote:

> You were dead because of your sins and because your sinful nature was not yet cut away. Then God made you alive with Christ,

for he forgave all our sins. He canceled the record of the charges against us and took it away by nailing it to the cross.

A little further on, Paul wrote,

Since God chose you to be the holy people he loves, you must clothe yourselves with tenderhearted mercy, kindness, humility, gentleness, and patience. Make allowance for each other's faults, and forgive anyone who offends you. Remember, the Lord forgave you, so you must forgive others. (Colossians 3:12–13)

This is majorly significant and will seriously affect our relationship with our Father, so we can't miss this! Our sins were forgiven in Christ, and we were taken from the point of death to life in Christ—*only* in Christ. Now, as followers of Christ, as extravagantly loved and chosen children, we are told to make another choice. Not only must we choose the narrow road—the road less traveled—but we must clothe ourselves differently from other travelers. The blue jeans God asks us now to clothe ourselves with are "tenderhearted mercy, kindness, humility, gentleness, and patience." And, as we wear this clothing, we will live a life of forgiveness.

Again, forgiveness is recognizing the full power of those wrongs and the ugliness of them, but then releasing the hold they have on us and allowing them to sit at the foot of the cross where Jesus carried our own offenses. Jesus paid the price for *all* of it. We must choose the narrow road and pack the clothes needed for the journey.

⋯⋯⋯⋯ REFLECTION ⋯⋯⋯⋯

The act of forgiveness is serious spiritual heart surgery. It can't be done in our own power and it rarely happens instantly. This narrow road is difficult and the clothes of mercy, kindness, humility, gentleness, and patience must be put on regularly—daily, and even sometimes moment by moment. Are we willing to wear this new wardrobe? Let's take time now to talk with our Father. We need to thank him for running toward us and pouring his love and mercy out on us! Our hearts need to thank Jesus for fully carrying our sin on the cross. This would be a great moment to ask God to help us release our own guilt, shame, fear, and unforgiveness to him, and then to help us also release to him those who have wounded us. Are we ready to take this necessary and important step?

Seven

...

LIVING IN HUMILITY

Most of us have heard the story of Jesus's birth hundreds of times, whether straight from scripture, watching a Christmas play, or even hearing Linus's recitation in *A Charlie Brown Christmas*. We can believe this is either the most ridiculous, silly story ever told or the most amazing, wonderful, and incredible event in all of history. I don't think there is an in-between on this. I mean, this is the stuff that people write about in fairy tales or the stuff that changes human history.

It begins with a poor, young girl from a small, persecuted, minority group who has an encounter with an angel and becomes pregnant while not married. She says that she has never even had sex with a man. Yeah, right. And even more incredible—this baby boy is God's Son.

What! This is either ridiculously absurd—or it's incredibly amazing! It's certainly not just a nice children's story.

Our culture has avoided the real issues of this story for so long that it's easy to become numb to the radical truth—even if we are followers of Jesus. The bottom line is that this is not a sweet story. This is a scandalous story! This is a story full of pain and brokenness. This is a story in which a child is born, the family is humiliated, and those who know about the boy's birth either ridicule the mother and father or want to kill the baby! The only people who seem to know who the baby really is turn out to be a group of uneducated shepherds, straight from the fields, who claim that they were told about Jesus by an army of angels. (For the full story, read Luke 1:1—2:20.)

Either this story is a childish fantasy or it should rock us to the point that no matter what is going on in our lives, we are able to sing and dance and celebrate. Because, if this story is true, there is real hope for us! If this story is true, there is joy beyond our brokenness, and peace in the midst of any circumstance. If this story is true, we have something to live for and there is a Presence with us more glorious than we could ever imagine.

I'm a believer, and as I reflect on this story, I am struck by—even blown away by—the humility of God. Even to describe God as humble feels a little awkward, because humility seems to be a very earthly and human term.

I mean—God is eternal, unlimited, and unequaled. Where does humility fit into that? But one of the messages that I think the birth of Jesus conveys the loudest is that of humility. I keep pondering this and arriving at the same conclusion. One of the strong messages of the gospel is that Jesus Christ entered the world, lived, and died in humility.

We can glimpse this idea through the eyes of Isaiah, that great blue jean–wearing prophet of Israel. Isaiah lived about seven hundred years before Jesus lived. He heard and saw things from God and spoke to the nation of Israel when they were in the midst of tough times. Their hearts had wandered far from God, and they were being overrun by the power and brute force of the Assyrian and Babylonian empires. But they still didn't humble themselves and turn wholeheartedly back to God. In the midst of this, God—through his prophet Isaiah—began to unveil a coming day when the people's hearts would be reawakened and brute force would not rule the world. Instead, the world would be ruled in humility by someone much greater. In Isaiah 7 we read these words:

> Then Isaiah said, "Listen well, you royal family of David! Isn't it enough to exhaust human patience? Must you exhaust the patience of my God as well? All right then, the Lord himself

will give you the sign. Look! The virgin will conceive a child! She will give birth to a son and will call him Immanuel (which means 'God is with us')." (Isaiah 7:10–14)

This had specific meaning for King Ahaz and Israel in that day, but it went way beyond that to a meaning for all time. Seven hundred years before Mary made her outrageous claim, God had Isaiah write this down. Later on, God spoke again through Isaiah to make it clear that this child, Immanuel, would be born in misunderstanding, rejection, scandal, and hatred—and that he would give his life for our salvation and healing (see Isaiah 53). Jesus's birth on planet Earth was pregnant with meaning. He gave up all his glory in heaven and was willing to be wrapped in humanity and become completely helpless, vulnerable, and dependent on a teenage girl.

He gave up his divine privileges; he took the humble position of a slave and was born as a human being. When he appeared in human form, he humbled himself in obedience to God and died a criminal's death on a cross. (Philippians 2:7–8)

The King of kings and Lord of Lords invaded our planet, but in a way we would never expect. Very honestly, if I had been this King, I doubt I would have chosen a vulnerable condition. I think I would have rather come with all the armies of heaven, highlighted with exploding lightning and thunder. I imagine many of us would have been more inclined to say something like, "Listen, you small people are really messed up! You need to get on your knees and worship me, or I can just end this all right here and now!" Thankfully, that's not how the Son of God chose to come to us.

Isaiah 42 speaks more about Jesus coming in gentleness and humility:

> Look at my servant, whom I strengthen. He is my chosen one, who pleases me. I have put my Spirit upon him. He will bring justice to the nations. He will not shout or raise his voice in public. He will not crush the weakest reed or put out a flickering candle. (Isaiah 42:1–3)

Do we hear what Isaiah is saying? He says when Messiah comes—when God comes to us—he is not going to shout, he is not going to demand, he is not going to wield all of the force that is fully his. Isaiah calls us "bruised or weak reeds" and "flickering candles." Think about a reed that's bent so low that if any more pressure is applied, it will snap right off. Isaiah says that when the Messiah comes in his humility, tenderness, compassion, and kindness, he will be careful not to add more pressure to snap that reed. Instead, he will lift and heal it. Think about a flickering candle with barely enough wick or oxygen to stay lit—more smoke than flame—and just struggling to hold on. One little puff and it would be history. But when the Messiah comes in all of his humility, tenderness, compassion, and kindness, he will not snuff out that flickering wick. Instead, he will guard and refuel it and breathe it back to life.

The truth is, Jesus came to us in the most humble way possible. We are those bruised reeds and flickering candles, aren't we? We have fears, insecurities, financial pressures, relational problems, depression, addiction, desperate grief, brokenness, shame—whatever life has heaped upon us or we have heaped upon ourselves. Jesus comes to us in the midst of our struggles, and—instead of demanding, shouting, and rebuking (as he certainly has the power and right to do)—he comes tenderly, offering himself to us. He comes to strengthen and heal; he comes to light a fresh fire within us.

It's crucial that we not mistake his humility for weakness. Jesus is no wimp. He is the King of kings! This is the Master of the cosmos, the One from whom life itself flows! His is unlimited power and authority! He is a beautiful contradiction of ultimate strength and power mixed with tenderness, mercy, and compassion. In this, Jesus shows us that true power is wrapped in vulnerability.

That's the beginning of the story, but the end will be even more remarkable. The next time Jesus comes to planet Earth, he will crack the sky! In Revelation 19:11–16, we are told that he will come with a vast army of heaven, with full authority and dominion. But even in all of his rightful display of glory, he will still come in humility. In Hebrews 13:8, we are told that "Jesus Christ is the same yesterday, today, and forever." The humble, glorious warrior, king, servant, Messiah—Immanuel—is present with us today. How will we respond to him?

·················· **REFLECTION** ··················

Life is beautiful and life is hard. In the hard times, if we are honest, we realize that our strength, intellect, and abilities are not enough. Our lives often reflect a "weak or bruised reed" or "flickering wick." In these moments and all moments, we have Jesus, the King of kings in all of his glory—and all of his humility. We are invited to let his compassion, tenderness, strength, and mighty power overwhelm us today. We are also asked to follow him and live our lives, all of our lives, in humility. Humility is really strength, not weakness. Let's take a few moments to bow our hearts in humility before the humble and mighty King of kings. What are some steps we can start taking in order to live with greater humility before God and others?

Eight

...

LIVING WITH
FEWER WORDS

I went to college and graduate school back in the 1980s and early 1990s. (My children refer to that as the Dark Ages.) I studied a lot of the biological sciences and also psychology. During the time when I was in school, a popular study came out about the number of words that men and women use during the course of one day. That study, which held up until recently, said that on average women use twenty thousand words every day, and on average men use seven thousand words each day. In addition to those seven thousand words, men use a variety of grunts and noises. Few disagreed with these findings—there may have even been a few grunts of approval heard from the men.

I had no trouble believing the report because I am the youngest of six children, and the only boy. So I grew up in a house with, let's see—an average of one hundred thousand words spoken by my sisters each day! I could believe that. And I'm sure if you ask my sisters, they will tell you that they heard a lot of grunts and weird noises from their brother. This study just backed up much of what our culture taught—that women like to talk and men don't.

A more recent study, however, with solid statistical validity, reports that there's not too much of a difference in the number of words men and women speak. These researchers found that on average, men and women both use about sixteen thousand words each day. The difference comes mainly in how males and females use language: men generally use words to solve problems and speak about issues, while women generally use words more for comprehension, and on a deeper, more relational level. Honestly, this now makes even more sense to me, because the truth is, I probably talk more than all my sisters combined (but please don't tell them I said that).

Importantly, the researchers dropped off the extreme highs and lows so they didn't skew the results. There were some men who were found to speak less than five

hundred words a day. (Do you know anyone like that?)
On the high end, there actually was one guy who spoke
forty-five thousand words in one day. (Wow! Was anyone really listening?) As it turns out, I think I married
this wonderful-but-talkative man's daughter. Thankfully,
she is more in the sixteen thousand–word-per-day range.

Here's what I thought about as I read these studies:
At the end of the day, it really doesn't matter how many
words we speak. What matters is how much we *say*.
During one of my trips to our mission sites in Liberia,
I noticed a large billboard in the capital city of Monro-
via that said Talk Less, Say More. That message got my
attention and is seared upon my brain.

Many of us use a whole lot of words, but they often
contain very little meaningful content. Some of us never
seem to get where we need to with our communication.
We never say what really needs to be said. I remember
this certain physiology class that I took in graduate
school. I had a bright professor and we had a good relationship. I honestly hadn't studied very well for the first
part of this course. At midterm, he gave us the kind of
exam that many dread—it was a one-question essay. No
multiple choice, no true or false. No chance to guess my
way to a halfway decent score. Just one question for the
full weight of an exam. With a heavy heart, I read that
question and I knew that I didn't have a good handle on

the answer. So what did I do? I wrote pages and pages of somewhat-related nonsense!

I hoped that somehow if I could use a lot of words, the professor might believe I knew what I was talking about. So I wrote this ridiculously long essay. I think I might have even convinced myself that I knew what I was talking about. When the exams were finally returned, the professor's note simply said, "Hey Rob, why didn't you just say you didn't know the answer?" Haha—I'll never forget that. He didn't waste words on me. He went straight to the point—which is what I should have done.

I believe all of us would be so much better off in life if we were simply willing to admit what we don't know rather than trying to excuse, theologize, philosophize, or vocalize using long, extended verbiage when, bottom line, sometimes we just don't know. Very often, we waste a great deal of time saying things that don't mean anything, while the words that need to be spoken remain unsaid.

Consider Jesus's style of communication. What kind of example did he set for us? There is a very important conversation between Jesus and a well-educated teacher of the law of Israel—a man named Nicodemus—recorded in the gospel of John. Nicodemus came to Jesus one night. He began to tell Jesus about how clear it was that he was sent to them with the wisdom and power of God. Jesus gave a rather strange response, saying, "I tell you the truth, unless you are born again, you cannot see the Kingdom of God" (John 3:3). The confused Nicodemus responded, "How can an old man go back into his mother's womb and be born again?" (John 3:4) Jesus went on to talk to Nicodemus about the difference between being born physically through a mother and father and being born spiritually through the mercy and power of God. He made it clear that eternal life requires not just physical birth but also being born again by the Spirit. All of this confused Nicodemus. Jesus went on to say,

> No one has ever gone to heaven and returned. But the Son of Man has come down from heaven. And as Moses lifted up the bronze snake on a pole in the wilderness, so the Son of Man must be lifted up, so that everyone who believes in him will have eternal life.
>
> For God loved the world so much that he gave his one and only Son, so that everyone who believes in him will not perish but have eternal life. God sent his Son into the world not to judge the world, but to save the world through him. (For the full discussion, see John 3:1–21.)

Nicodemus was very well educated. He was an expert in the law of Moses and the entire Old Testament

(Hebrew scriptures), as well as the teachings of the rabbis. He came to Jesus, at night, for various reasons.
Perhaps he just wanted one-on-one time with Jesus,
or it could be that he didn't want to be seen speaking with him, considering his societal position or the
soul-searching he was doing. In any case, he came. He
came because he had heard Jesus teaching and knew
that Jesus was different. Perhaps he had seen some of
the miracles Jesus performed, and saw power that he
had never witnessed before. Possibly it was because
there was some yearning deep within his heart, but he
was not yet willing to admit it.

Nonetheless, Nicodemus came to Jesus. He opened
the conversation on the surface with some polite flattery,
which was sure to start them off well: "Jesus, you are a
godsend, and God is obviously with you." But Jesus's
response seems to have no connection whatsoever to
what Nicodemus just said. It's as if he wasn't even listening. But actually, Jesus was listening below the surface of
Nicodemus's words. Jesus knew what Nicodemus needed
on the deepest level. He wasn't going to waste words,
and went straight for the heart: "Let's say what needs to
be said. Nicodemus, you need to be born again."

Nicodemus was shocked. He was floating comfortably on the surface of the water, and Jesus just yanked
him under. "Jesus, what are you talking about? How

can I crawl back inside the womb of my mother?" Jesus assures Nicodemus that he's speaking not about a physical rebirth, but about a spiritual one. Jesus knew why Nicodemus had really come: not because he wanted to acknowledge the teachings of Jesus or pat him on the back, but because there was a hunger in his heart and he was drawn to Jesus. Nicodemus knew there was something very different, but he wasn't willing or able to fully admit that. Jesus wasn't interested in small talk. He chose to "speak less, but say more," and he went straight to the deepest level of Nicodemus's heart.

This is how Jesus communicates, including with us today. Many of us respond like I did on my physiology exam—words, words, and more words—and we never admit our need or lack of understanding. We struggle to get to the point and say what needs to be spoken, to God or to the people in our lives. For us, it's time to speak less and say more.

Many people choose to spend much of their time watching the weather or the news or listening to talk radio. News programs and talk radio are big business, and so they seek to entertain and to keep our attention. I do believe it's helpful and important to be informed and stay aware of cultural trends and national and world events, but then as followers of Jesus, we need to live the gospel and share the gospel. We are called to go out and make the news instead of spending all our time reading about or watching or brooding over what's wrong in our world.

Each day offers us the opportunity to quiet down and listen to God and to others and then to speak what needs to be spoken. We have the opportunity to dive below the surface to the heart of the matter in our marriages, in our relationships with our kids, and with everyone else in our lives. We can be like Nicodemus, comfortably floating on the surface—but Jesus didn't come to hang out there with us. He didn't come shouting or demanding or speaking endless words, but he did come to say what needed to be said. Jesus came in love. He came to make a difference. He came for our hearts.

In the gospel of Luke, chapter 5, we see another example of Jesus "speaking less, but saying more." Jesus has become known for his powerful teaching and for healing people. He's in a house jam-packed with people, and there's a paralyzed man outside being carried by friends who want to take him in to Jesus to be healed (those are good friends!). These friends will do whatever it takes, so they go up on the roof and pull off the thatching, and lower their friend right down in front of Jesus. Now that's impressive. Jesus doesn't waste any time. He speaks straight to his heart and says, "Young man, your sins are forgiven."

I imagine that young man thinking, "What! I came

to be healed, not forgiven." The people watching in the crowd, including the religious leaders, were outraged! How dare Jesus offer forgiveness! They knew that only God can forgive sins. Who did he think he was? But Jesus knew this man needed more than just physical healing; he needed healing of the paralysis of his soul, and because Jesus was God, he gave the man all that he could offer him. Jesus healed his soul and his body that day. He knew exactly what the man needed to hear— and that's what he spoke into his life.

Another significant conversation was between Jesus and his friend Peter, at the end of the gospel of John. We discussed this a little bit in chapter 1. As a reminder, Peter had denied Jesus three times and was obviously struggling with that fact. He was carrying guilt and shame—the overwhelming emotions of how unworthy he was for betraying his friend and Lord. But Jesus does not leave him in that dark place. Instead, he looks right at Peter and speaks what needs to be spoken.

We've already discussed the multiple times Jesus asked Peter whether he loved him and was truly his friend. Equally important, though, is what was said after each of Peter's responses. Jesus said, "Feed my lambs; take care of my sheep; feed my sheep."

Ultimately, for Peter, this conversation meant restoration. Jesus placed a calling back into Peter's life, essentially saying, "You are my disciple again. I'm asking you to serve me, Peter. We're good." But Jesus was also speaking in the presence of the other disciples, who knew Peter's guilt, and who now witnessed Jesus restoring Peter. I'm not sure they would have allowed Peter back into the inner circle had Jesus not done that—I certainly would have struggled with that. Sometimes when we affirm another person, it is more meaningful to give that affirmation in front of others—in front of witnesses. By doing this, we bring others on board and we encourage them to follow our lead.

As we strive to follow Jesus, it's important to follow his example in this. We also need to say the words that need to be said—to use our words for healing. Some of us understand the pain of not hearing what our hearts long to hear. Some of us in our relationships are starving because we don't say simple (but difficult) words like "I love you," "I forgive you," "I'm proud of you," or "I'm sorry." We splash around on the surface in our own arrogance or discomfort and refuse to dive in where we need to. We need to think about our communication the way we do our blue jeans. It doesn't have to be stylish and sophisticated. It should be real and comfortable. Jesus kept it real with what he said and did, and as we follow him, we should also.

Some of our children are crying inside and acting

out because we are not looking in our children's eyes and saying, "I'm proud of you; I love you." Very often (and I mean *very* often), I have needed to tell my children, "I'm sorry." I ask their forgiveness for speaking too quickly or too harshly or for reacting before taking the time to listen and understand. Some would say that I'm the parent and need to stand in my authority, as if humility were weakness, but we've already seen the power of God in humility, haven't we.

There are people in our lives who are withering because we prefer to make noise instead of speaking words of hope, truth, life, love, or healing to them. In our stubbornness, we often think we need to wait on someone else to make the first move, say the first word. There's no time for that. It's time to make this change. It's time we speak less and say more.

Our own relationship with God could be suffering because we are not willing to speak to God the words he is waiting for us to say. We are not willing to say, "I'm sorry," or, "I need you, Lord; I'm desperate." Instead, we make excuses like, "He knows what I'm thinking, why do I need to say it?" And we rationalize or stuff things inside rather than just coming clean and saying to the Lord what we most need to say—"Forgive me."

In Proverbs chapter 10, verse 19, it says, "Too much talk leads to sin. Be sensible and keep your mouth shut."

How's that for a strong word? This is a strong reminder that the more we speak, the more likely we are to put our foot in our mouth or say things we will regret. But God also speaks to us about the importance and potential benefits of our words. In Proverbs chapter 12, verses 14 and 18, we are reminded, "Wise words bring many benefits. . . . Some people make cutting remarks, but the words of the wise bring healing." Instead of speaking words that wound, we have the opportunity today to speak words of hope, truth, life, love, and healing.

I remember the phrase we used to say as children— "Sticks and stones may break my bones, but words will never hurt me." That is so far from the truth, as we've all experienced. Words can't break bones, but they certainly break hearts—and hearts are much harder to heal. Words have the power to destroy lives or the power to give life. Let's speak less and say more and choose to be more thoughtful about the content and impact of our words.

·················· **REFLECTION** ··················

Jesus always speaks to us the words we need to hear. His loving and truthful words are already recorded for us in the gospels. Will we listen? Will we respond? Instead of long, empty essays, excuses, or silence, what do we really need to say to God today?

Let's also consider who we may have wounded with our words or with our silence. Who is it that is longing just to hear some life-giving words from us? It's time to go for the heart, break the silence, cut through the excess fluff, and speak what needs to be spoken.

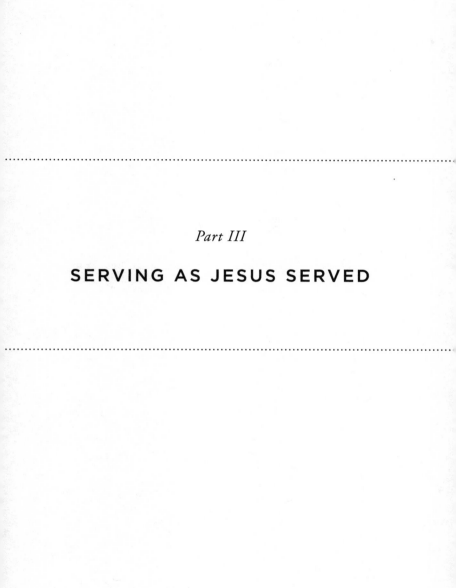

Part III

SERVING AS JESUS SERVED

Nine

...

SERVING GOD

I was in the store recently looking for some Band-Aids. When I looked at the shelves, I almost became frozen with how many choices there were. Band-Aids now come in an endless range of sizes and shapes and colors. They even come with superhero images (Superman is my personal favorite!). But at the end of the day—they all have the same function. Band-Aids are great to cover and help protect superficial cuts and scrapes but not too helpful with deep wounds.

In life, however, our wounds and heartache often cut real deep. So we can be grateful that Jesus came to do much more than put a Superman Band-Aid on our hearts. His purpose always goes much deeper, for our healing, and is more like a heart transplant. Jesus came to earth for serious business. He also isn't satisfied to give our spirits a minor adjustment; Jesus came to give us a new spirit and to even place his Spirit within us (see Ezekiel 11:19; John 14:15–17).

In the gospel of John, chapter 1, we read the announcement that everyone who truly believes in Jesus and receives his salvation becomes a child of God. One of the things this new relationship brings us is a fresh freedom to live and serve as Jesus did. It's so important to understand that freedom isn't just about being able to do whatever we want. Freedom is about finally being able to choose to do what we should do—the right thing. This isn't about rules and regulations. This is about real change from the inside out. It's not that we now have any greater value than those around us, but that something radical has happened and we really do become different. The Bible describes how, as we follow Jesus, we are rescued from darkness and slavery and brought into light and freedom (Colossians 1:13–14). This is why Jesus came. The gospel is that good! As we walk this narrow road less traveled with Jesus, we find a growing desire and ability to live differently in small and large ways. There will often be challenges, but Jesus is so faithful and his love has set us free.

When we look at Jesus, we see that his heart was

always to honor and serve God his Father. Through the Bible we know much about the birth of Jesus, and then his life and ministry beginning at age thirty. But we only read one story about him as a child. In this story, Jesus was twelve years old and was traveling with his parents from Nazareth to Jerusalem for the annual Passover celebration. They had been traveling in a large group, and when they left to return to Nazareth, they found that Jesus had wandered off and was not with them (sounds like my son). They walked back to Jerusalem and finally found Jesus in the temple, in deep discussion with the religious teachers there. Mary and Joseph had been so worried about young Jesus. When they told their son how concerned they had been and how frantically they had been searching for him, Jesus replied, "Didn't you know I must be about my Father's business?" (For the full story, read Luke 2:41–52.)

Later, as Jesus began to teach and heal people and perform all kinds of miracles, he said this: "I tell you the truth, the Son can do nothing by himself. He does only what he sees the Father doing. Whatever the Father does, the Son also does" (John 5:19). In these statements and through how he lived, we see that the heart of Jesus was always to be faithful in serving God his Father. As we seek to follow Jesus, this will become our heart too. We will begin to see the moments of our day as opportunities to honor and serve God. Like that favorite pair of jeans, this purpose becomes our sweet spot and comfort zone, which can and should permeate our work, our recreation, and our relationships. Serving God isn't about becoming a priest or pastor or missionary (although it can lead there for some of us). It's simply about seeing, as Jesus did, all of our life as an opportunity to honor God's heart and bring honor to him.

Around AD 320 there was a group of Roman soldiers known as the Thundering Legion. They were stationed in Armenia, in a region that is modern-day Turkey. These soldiers were known for being effective and fearless. They had also come to be known for being faithful followers of Jesus Christ and having hearts to honor him even as soldiers.

It was during this time that the Roman emperor Constantine professed faith in Jesus Christ and was declaring Christianity to be legal instead of a religion against the state. Constantine had control over the western empire, but there was another emperor named Licinius who controlled the eastern empire. He hated Christians and enjoyed throwing them to the lions or lighting them on fire as human torches, just for sport.

Licinius declared that all soldiers under his rule must renounce faith in Jesus and bow and worship him and the Roman gods. The edict was sent everywhere, including to the Thundering Legion. All forty of these fearless men sought to be good soldiers and honor their leaders, but they refused to worship anyone or anything except Jesus. The governor offered to give these soldiers money and rewards if they would bow in worship, but they refused. He then threatened them with torture and death, but they still refused to bow. After many attempts to persuade these soldiers by promise and threat, it is recorded that a leader among them named Camdidus responded to the governor,

> You offer us money that remains behind and glory that fades away. You seek to make us friends of the Emperor, but alienate us from the true King. We desire one gift, the crown of righteousness. We are anxious for one glory, the glory of the heavenly kingdom. We love honors, those of heaven. You threaten fearful torments and call our godliness a crime, but you will not find us fainthearted or attached to this life or easily stricken with terror. For the love of God, we are prepared to endure any kind of torture.

Because the Thundering Legion refused to deny Jesus, these forty men were stripped naked and marched

to the middle of a frozen lake to painfully and slowly die.
They were offered the chance to leave the ice and find
warmth and comfort at any moment if they were willing
to change their minds and renounce their faith. Through
the night, they stood and prayed and sang and encour-
aged one another. After many torturous hours, one of
the men couldn't take it any longer. He renounced Jesus
and ran off the lake. Watching all of this and seeing the
one man abandon the group, one of the soldiers standing guard at the shore threw off his clothes and joined
the men on the ice, declaring, "I am a Christian." By
morning, forty brave and loving followers of Jesus were
dead. They sought to honor and serve God faithfully to
the end and were now fully alive with him.

Whenever I think about these soldiers I get a little
choked up. They were strong and courageous warriors
but they were human. The pressure and temptation they
faced was so great, but they would not deny Jesus. For
them, the amazing gospel of Jesus was far greater than
anything on earth. I am so inspired by their faith and
strength and love. I think about how easy it would have
been for them to compromise and bow and take the
easy way. But they stood strong and their example has
inspired thousands through the centuries to also stand
strong when serving Jesus is extremely hard.

Daniel was another man who stood strong and

sought to honor God in all of his life. While just a teen-ager, Daniel was taken from his family and homeland and marched to Babylon as a prisoner of war (this was in the seventh century BC). He was then put through intensive reprogramming and trained extensively with the history, language, literature, art, and religion of his captors. But Daniel never forgot who he was and who his God was. He chose to trust and serve God in the midst of this hideous storm. Daniel rose quickly as a trusted political leader, and the king placed him in a position of high honor and authority. This didn't sit well with many of the other leaders, who were jealous and didn't like Daniel because he was a Jew and a foreigner. They looked for a character flaw but couldn't find any. "[Daniel] was faithful, always responsible, and completely trustworthy" (Daniel 6:4). So these administrators went to the king (Darius) and convinced him to sign into law that, for thirty days, everyone must worship only him with a penalty of death to those who did not obey. What did Daniel do? He didn't change. He stayed faithful. He kept praying and serving his God. The king gave the order for Daniel to be arrested and thrown into the den of lions and said, "May your God, whom you serve so faithfully, rescue you" (Daniel 6:16). The rest, as they say, is history.

There are many biblical, historical, and contemporary

examples for those who have faithfully served God and found it to be the joy and sweet spot of their lives. Many faithful women and men have been willing to put their lives on the line, and many have been killed for their choice. The big choices—those monumental stands—are often very clear when we come face-to-face with them. It's the smaller, daily choices that can be more subtle and lead to a gradual fading away from serving only the Lord. It can be very tempting to allow other passions to slowly take our heart's desire away from walking with him, even while worshiping him.

Toward the end of the first century AD, Jesus—through a vision to a man named John—sent a message to seven churches in Asia Minor (same area where the Thundering Legion were later to be stationed). These letters are contained in Revelation, the final book of the New Testament. Jesus's words were often encouraging and filled with gratitude, but his letter to the church in Laodicea stated this: "I know all the things you do, that you are neither hot nor cold. I wish that you were one or the other! But since you are like lukewarm water, neither hot nor cold, I will spit you out of my mouth!" (Revelation 3:15–16)

Jesus is essentially saying, "Whatever you're drinking, I don't want it, because you have lost your passion to love and serve God." He clearly isn't impressed with our lip service—good deeds apart from surrendered hearts and lives. We can't really serve God and ourselves—or anyone or anything else—at the same time.

One final word on this: Jesus warns his followers about not allowing the love of money to take away our heart to love and serve God.

> No one can serve two masters. For you will hate one and love the other; you will be devoted to one and despise the other. You cannot serve both God and money. (Matthew 6:24)

This is an important word for all of us no matter what our financial status is. Our culture is so much about money and material things. We need to guard our hearts and keep our desires in check. Our resources, no matter how large or how limited, can be used very selfishly or for great good, depending on who and what owns our heart.

·················· **REFLECTION** ··················

In the moments and days of our lives—who are we serving, and who owns our heart? Where is our real passion and desire? Are we willing to be like the Thundering Legion or like Daniel in our day? Is it our primary desire in all of life to love and serve our Father God? Do we find gratitude and contentment within our hearts? Let's ask the Lord to help us not be lukewarm and instead be passionate about serving him in both the small and the great areas of daily living.

Ten

...

SERVING OTHERS

Giovanni grew up in central Italy with a great love for life. He enjoyed nice clothes, good food and drink, singing, and dancing. He was expected to take over his father's fabric business and do well as a businessman. But then war came and Giovanni joined the army. He was a prisoner of war at the age of twenty and grew up very quickly in that year of imprisonment. Giovanni returned home with a radically different perspective on life—himself, others, and God. He believed God wanted him to provide for the repair of his local church building, which had fallen into ruins, so he sold his horse and some fabric from his father's shop and gave the money to the priest. Giovanni's father was not happy and took his son to the bishop to be straightened out. Instead, Giovanni removed his clothes—all of them (I don't necessarily recommend this)—and chose to walk away from the comforts connected to his family's wealth. From this point forward, he embraced God as his Father, and a life of serving others that for him included poverty. Giovanni had a radical faith (I highly recommend this!).

Giovanni's father had nicknamed him Francesco (or Francis, in English) at a very early age, and this was the name most knew him by. The town in Italy he was from was called Assisi. This Giovanni was Francis of Assisi. Maybe you have heard of him? This completely sold-out rebel for Christ has become legendary for his determination to follow Jesus with radical simplicity and servitude. Thousands have followed his example. Francis lived a life of complete abandon. He didn't get too attached to the stuff of this world and was a faithful follower of Jesus until his death. He served the lepers, gave to the poor, and took the good news of Jesus to other nations. Interestingly, it is said that Francis was so gentle that he actually was able to communicate with the garden animals (very cool). One of the well-known quotations attributed to Francis is "Preach the gospel at all times and, when necessary, use words." I like this quote not because I don't think words are important (they are!) but because the way we live outshouts the words we speak.

Certainly Francis spoke the gospel of Jesus to many, but it was his daily life and acts of service that had the greatest impact on those around him.

The prophet Isaiah gives us great insight into God's idea of worship. He's not impressed with external religious habits (when they are empty-hearted) and asks us instead to worship him in action:

> Free those who are wrongly imprisoned; lighten the burden of those who work for you.
>
> Let the oppressed go free, and remove the chains that bind people.
>
> Share your food with the hungry, and give shelter to the homeless.
>
> Give clothes to those who need them, and do not hide from relatives who need your help. . . .
>
> Feed the hungry, and help those in trouble. (Isaiah 58:6–7, 10)

It's clear, throughout scripture, that if God's love is alive in us, then our love will also be alive toward helping and serving others. We can't love God without loving others. We can't serve God without serving others. Francis knew that and lived it, and we need to also.

As we attempt to live out Isaiah 58 as Francis

did—and, more importantly, as Jesus did—we can bring these verses into modern application. If we are bosses, managers, or leaders, God tells us to "lighten the burden" of those who work for us. Certainly, the work has to be done, but we can make it our goal to encourage and reward others while being humble leaders who are kind and enjoyable to work with. We can do our best not to overload or be an overlord to those who work under our direction.

Letting the "oppressed go free" and removing the "chains that bind people" means that we will take an active stand against racism or slavery in whatever form we find it. It also may simply require that we listen and give wise counsel to a broken heart, or walk alongside a friend struggling with addiction or stuck in grief. As we encounter people who are bound by physical, emotional, or spiritual chains, we are called to be freedom fighters on their behalf.

Today, we can share food with the hungry by buying a gift card to a grocery store for a struggling friend or family, giving a neighbor a ride to the local food bank, or inviting a lonely widow over for supper. Maybe the "hunger" is spiritual, so we could help "feed" them with friendship, prayer, or a personal invitation to attend church with us.

"Giving shelter to the homeless" might mean offering

a room in our house to a friend or family until they are back on their feet. It might also mean serving at or supporting a shelter in our town or city. God also says that we should be "giving clothes to those who need them." If someone really needs clothing, there's probably some extra hanging in our closet, or there's a department store or thrift store nearby we can take him or her to. Often it seems easier to help a complete stranger than someone we know well. When it comes to helping family members, God knows how particularly hard it can be. He specifically tells us not to "hide" from them. Pride and our relational history can sometimes affect our desire to step in. But God says we can't turn our back on our own flesh and blood.

Jesus shared some startling words that are recorded in the gospel of Matthew. He actually said that when we feed someone who is hungry, clothe someone who is naked, care for someone who is sick, or visit someone who is in prison—we are caring not just for that person but also for him! (See Matthew 25:31–36.) That's an overwhelming perspective. If we are going to walk with Jesus and carry the gospel in blue jeans, we really need to open our eyes and look around. Opportunities to serve are everywhere.

In living out our faith in Jesus by serving those he places in our path, we are able to practice our "speak less, say more" principle. The number of people whose lives most of us have the opportunity to speak deeply into on a day-to-day basis is very few—we only have so much time and energy. Often, though, we impact many more than those we go eye-to-eye with. People are watching. The neighbors see us in the driveway playing basketball with the kids; the people behind us in line see how we interact with the cashier; and the people at the table next to us overhear our conversations with friends and family. Anytime we're in public, we have the opportunity to serve others by splashing the love and kindness of Jesus on them.

I am privileged to travel often to other nations where we've established mission programs. During trips to India, my life was deeply impacted by a humble servant of Jesus named Azariah. Azariah walked with Jesus along the dusty roads of South India for over fifty years. He never took a salary but was used by God to establish churches, schools, orphanages, and extensive ministries to the elderly, poor, sick, widows, and orphans. I never saw Azariah walk past a person in need without doing what he could to help. He was a man who used few words to say a lot and in his kindness shared the gospel and helped others "consider Jesus." Azariah was filled with the love of Jesus. He repeated often the words that are attributed to Mother Teresa (whom he had met with many times), "Not all of us can do great things. But we can all do small things with great love." His example has deeply affected my life.

I attended graduate school in Kentucky. I'm a Jersey boy but I was drawn toward southern hospitality. My wife, Debra, is from Kentucky, where this kindness and hospitality are more prominent in the culture. People seem to more naturally smile and offer a friendly greeting to others—even strangers passing on the street. When we were married and Deb moved to New Jersey with me, she had a difficult time adjusting to the more "aggressive" culture. She said it felt like everyone was mad at her. People sometimes even yelled during friendly conversations (you northeasterners get it), and this was hard for her to adjust to.

And now, after over twenty years of Jersey living, Deb recognizes that although the South as a culture is often friendlier on the surface (which is nice), the northern folk perhaps simply wear their emotions more on the surface and are more "honest" in their expressions (work with me here). Deb has come to appreciate the friendships she's grown by winning people's trust and earning a smile from a frowning face. People long for kindness—in every culture—but it must be authentic to win a heart, and most people know when it's real and when it's not. So we can't perform. We need to be the real deal. Our faith must come alive in our actions.

What good is it, dear brothers and sisters, if you say you have faith but don't show it by your actions? Can that kind of faith save anyone? Suppose you see a brother or sister who has no food or clothing, and you say, "Good-bye and have a good day; stay warm and eat well"—but then you don't give that person any food or clothing. What good does that do? So you see, faith by itself isn't enough. Unless it produces good deeds, it is dead and useless. . . . We are shown to be right with God by what we do, not by faith alone. . . . Just as the body is dead without breath, so also faith is dead without good works. (James 2:14–17, 24, 26)

When a friend or stranger is in real need, our gut reaction can be to simply say, "I'll pray for you." After all, we know prayer is a powerful, God-given tool. We are told to never stop praying (1 Thessalonians 5:17). So, sincerely said, this doesn't have to be a meaningless answer. But God requires more of us than that. We are also commanded to meet the real needs of that friend or stranger as best we can.

I am privileged to be a pastor at Zarephath Christian Church. Our church has a very active outreach and social action ministry. We offer food, clothing, counseling, and medical treatment. We often assist with rent and utilities to keep families afloat. Many in our church volunteer resources, time, and energy to pour into the lives of the needy, and it's beautiful how these ministries have grown and how they touch so many lives. I interact with people all the time who may not believe that Jesus is Lord (yet) and who aren't interested in the music or messages and don't attend the church, but who have been deeply impacted by the demonstrated love they hear about or have encountered through our church. Francis of Assisi would call that sharing the gospel beyond words.

Serving others can be easy sometimes, but it can also be very stretching and get our blue jeans a little messy. That's okay. Our bodies and our souls (and our jeans) were designed to be stretched some. We can enjoy our moments and seasons of comfort, but we will miss out on so much beauty and meaning if we avoid God's opportunities for diving in to serve him by serving others.

················· **REFLECTION** ···················

People like Francis of Assisi, Azariah, and Mother
Teresa lived lives of radical simplicity and service to God and humanity. They allowed their
passionate love for Jesus to overflow in serving
others. How about us? Are we willing to let people hear the gospel through our words and feel
the gospel through our actions? As we seek to
live out the kind of worship God requires in Isaiah 58, which people come to mind? Who could
use our intervention, or food, shelter, clothing—
or just the simple kindness of someone who
cares? Let's ask the Lord to help us as we follow
him and serve others.

Eleven

...

SERVING UNIQUELY

I have really enjoyed watching my children grow and seeing their hearts, interests, and abilities develop. In some ways they are like me and in other ways they are like my wife, but they are also clearly unique in their own ways. There is no one else like them (or like you or me) on the planet. No one is a cookie-cutter person (and that's coming from a guy who really likes cookies!). And when it comes to walking with Jesus, there isn't anything "cookie cutter" about that either. We aren't clones or mutants—we are unique creations and dearly loved children.

Remember, when Jesus walked the earth he invited people to be his friends and follow him. This meant loving like him, living like him, and serving like him. If we are serious about walking with Jesus, we will—in some way—begin to imitate him. Each of us is unique and has our own distinctive strut, but there will also be similarities and shared traits among those who belong to Jesus.

Have you ever noticed how children usually walk and posture themselves after one of their parents? For many years I practiced as a physical therapist. I really enjoyed the study of anatomy and physiology and prided myself on my observation skills (my wife calls it staring). Often I would work with children who had gone through some type of neurological or orthopedic injury and help them along the road to recovery. This would sometimes include helping them learn to walk again. As a young clinician, I had an idealized perspective of correct mechanics and gait patterns and I would often work to correct what I observed as deviations or inefficiencies. It would at times be frustrating trying to break bad habits or mechanics, but then I would have my "a-ha" moment: I'd see the father or mother walk into the clinic. Their child walked just like them! What I thought was poor mechanics resulting from their trauma was actually their natural imitation of a parent.

Family patterns run strong, and if we are serious about walking with Jesus in this life, we will want to posture ourselves and walk like him. This is part of what it means in 1 John 1:6 when it says, "Those who say they live in God should live their lives as Jesus did."

Jesus said that he didn't come to be "served but to serve others and to give his life as a ransom for many" (Matthew 20:28). The servant's heart is something beautiful and truly countercultural. When you read through the New Testament, it's really humbling to see how these early followers of Jesus often identified themselves as "servants" or even "slaves" of the Lord, Jesus. See how these New Testament letters begin:

> This letter is from James, a slave of God and of the Lord Jesus Christ. (James 1:1)

> This letter is from Simon Peter, a slave and apostle of Jesus Christ. (2 Peter 1:1)

> This letter is from Jude, a slave of Jesus Christ. (Jude 1:1)

> This letter is from Paul, a slave of Christ Jesus, chosen by God to be an apostle and sent out to preach his Good News. (Romans 1:1)

None of these people were forced into slavery. It was their love for Jesus and his love in them that changed their hearts and gave them a sincere desire to walk with him and serve him in every way possible. It changed their identity as they became willing servants. This also brought them true freedom, vibrant life, and deep joy.

All of us have been shaped by genetics, nurture, and experience. God takes all these things as we give him our hearts. He then adds to the mix with other unique gifts and abilities to shape us to serve. Scripture talks about this in Romans 12:6—"In his grace, God has given us different gifts for doing certain things well." Things happen within us when we surrender our hearts to Jesus. When his Spirit comes into us, he brings a gift. (I love gifts!) It doesn't change our basic personality or take away our natural abilities, talents, and experience. Instead, God wants to use these things for his glory, to serve others; and he gives us what the Bible calls a spiritual gift that helps to pull these things together.

I don't think we should spend too much time trying to figure out what our main gift is. In my experience, it begins to evidence itself as we simply make ourselves available to the Lord. Jesus said that he came so we could be fully alive (John 10:10) and that God wants our lives to produce more life and be fruitful and have eternal impact (John 15:1–17). Our primary role is to make ourselves available to God and let him use our unique gifts, passions, and abilities as we keep our hearts surrendered to Jesus.

In 1 Corinthians 12:4–6 it says, "There are different

kinds of spiritual gifts, but the same Spirit is the source of them all. There are different kinds of service, but we serve the same Lord. God works in different ways, but it is the same God who does the work in all of us." All of us are wired distinctively and uniquely. God asks us to love him and serve him with what has been entrusted to us. That may mean some large-platform ministry, but mostly it means day-to-day and moment-by-moment being available to God and to others.

It is our tendency to compare our abilities and gifts with others, but this can be discouraging. Why can't I sing like her? Teach like him? Lead like her? Pray like him? We envy others' positions, talents, and abilities. This distraction often limits our ability to serve, because we lack confidence in who God has created us to be. Instead, we should embrace and enjoy our uniqueness. Our unique gifting and distinctive perspectives, brought together, can be much more enriching—and effective— to God's Kingdom work on earth.

The Bible reminds us that at the end of the day, all of our service must be done in love or it is worthless. We can have amazing gifts of talent, courage, and faith and outwardly do all the "right" things, but if our service is motivated by anything other than love, we are only making a bunch of noise and wasting our time (1 Corinthians 13:1–3).

In what ways do we have the opportunity each day to posture ourselves after Jesus and walk with a gait that looks like him? What do you think some of your natural strengths and weaknesses are? Since opening your heart to Jesus, have you been aware of a greater passion, desire, or ability in some area of your life? Let's spend some time talking with someone we know and trust and see what insight he or she may have for us regarding this. It's time for us to embrace the unique creations God has made each of us and to step out and serve and do what we were gifted to do. This is true freedom.

Twelve

...

SERVING WITH EXCELLENCE

I like shortcuts. I've always liked shortcuts. Through the years I can't even begin to tell you how many short-cuts I have taken—or how much extra time I have saved (okay—make that *added*) while doing the whole short-cut thing. But still, I'm usually game for trying one out. My wife and kids could tell you about some wild rides they have endured with me as I took them on another one of my famous "shortcuts" (I can hear their groans now). I'm finally coming to learn in life that shortcuts may often be adventurous but they are rarely effective.

My dad worked very hard with me on a similar lesson when I was a boy. He was a very good man and extremely patient (I really helped him develop this quality). Dad did his best to teach me a solid work ethic, to be faithful and reliable, to follow through and finish well and seek always to do things with excellence. Whether working on cars or mowing the lawn or doing my homework, he taught me that the job wasn't done until everything was finished, cleaned up, and put away. I always wanted to get creative and finish quickly (i.e., shortcut) so I could run out and play sports or hang with my friends. Dad taught me to leave things better than I found them. It frustrated him when I didn't give something my best, and thankfully, through his firm patience, some of this finally rubbed off on me.

God, our Father, is also very patient and kind with us. He loves us and has demonstrated that fact in so many ways—including, ultimately, in how he came to us and gave everything for us through his Son. As his children, and because we love him and belong to him, God asks us to now choose to live in ways that honor him.

In Colossians 3:17 we read this: "And whatever you do or say, do it as a representative of the Lord Jesus, giving thanks through him to God the Father." Kind of a radical perspective, don't you think? This means that in all things (working, eating, speaking, playing—in public, in private, in solitude, and in all relationships) we carry the name of Jesus and represent him. That's an incredible privilege and also an amazing responsibility that we need to take seriously.

Similar words are expressed in 1 Corinthians 10:31, where it says, "So whether you eat or drink, or whatever you do, do it all for the glory of God." There is never a moment where it is just about us. There are no segments or compartments of our life in which this calling does not apply.

The temptation for me and perhaps for you is to look for shortcuts. But in living for God and in serving others (and while driving in a car with me), we shouldn't take shortcuts. To be available, to give our best, to do it right and finish well— these things takes time and effort. Jesus expressed this with his words, "Do to others whatever you would like them to do to you. This is the essence of all that is taught in the law and the prophets" (Matthew 7:12). Jesus doesn't just ask this of us—first he modeled it for us. He was willing to be patient, loving, inconvenienced, stretched, vulnerable, and sacrificial in all things for us first.

Ultimately, in every aspect of our lives it is the Lord Jesus whom we are serving. God gives each of us opportunities and abilities to use for his glory and to help others. Along these lines, Paul wrote this to Christians in Rome:

> If God has given you the ability to prophesy,
> speak out with as much faith as God has given

you. If your gift is serving others, serve them well. If you are a teacher, teach well. If your gift is to encourage others, be encouraging. If it is giving, give generously. If God has given you leadership ability, take the responsibility seriously. And if you have a gift for showing kindness to others, do it gladly. (Romans 12:6–8)

Paul also reminded followers of Jesus to remember whom we are ultimately and always serving and that God deserves our best. "Work willingly at whatever you do, as though you were working for the Lord rather than for people" (Colossians 3:23).

·············· **REFLECTION** ··············

Where in life are we being tempted to take unhealthy or unloving shortcuts? How would some things specifically change in our work, habits, recreation, and relationships if we kissed shortcuts goodbye and committed to doing things wholeheartedly and with excellence before the Lord and others? Let's ask God to show us in what ways we can step up and serve him more out of love.

Thirteen

...

LOVING, LIVING, AND SERVING WHEN THE BLUE JEANS AREN'T COMFORTABLE

So back to those blue jeans . . .

The primary idea we have been considering is that if and as we truly bow our hearts to Jesus, walking with him here on this planet will be the great fit of our hearts. Our lives will be filled with intimacy and comfort—even better than the comfortable fit we get with our favorite pair of jeans. Our lives will be greatly characterized by this comfort, but not all the time. Just like it can sometimes be before our jeans are broken in, our walk with Jesus will not always feel great. Life is beautiful, but life is very hard.

This book has been in progress for many years. I laid it aside for quite a while because I thought, "There are already so many books that have been written by people much more wise and literate than I am. Does the world really need another one?" Then, a few years ago, a mentor of mine challenged me to reconsider and write it anyway. He said it was important to share what was on my heart even if only a few ever read it. Maybe, he said, it could deeply impact somebody in a way other books haven't. That motivated me. At first I preached a series of messages at my church entitled "Jesus, the Gospel, and Blue Jeans." (Sound familiar?) It included much of the material I have built upon in this book. My sister Teressa patiently listened and transcribed the messages to give me a solid start and a body of material to work with (thanks sis!). Even with all of this help, life gets very full, and I have alternated between starting and stopping, focus and distraction.

During the years of this writing process, life has changed much. Some of the change has been wonderful and some has been very difficult. Both of my parents and my father-in-law suffered through diseases that painfully took their lives. This was hard. There have been many other burdens and heartaches to carry over these years, many of them my own, many of them the burdens of our ministries around the world, and many belonging to others whom I am privileged to know and love and support. Three years ago, my dear, lifelong friend and brother-in-law was diagnosed with cancer. It quickly took him from us and into the full presence of Jesus. This was heartbreaking, and challenged and stretched my faith.

My hair now has much more gray in it and my body is starting to feel some wear and tear. I've learned lessons that only time and experience can bring. I still have much to learn and much growth ahead of me, but I have lived long enough to know how incredibly beautiful and joyful but also painful, disappointing, depressing, and gut-wrenching this life can be. Our faith can be stretched to its very limit and beyond as we cry out to the Lord, who at times seems silent and absent. Following Jesus does not take this from us, although it does bring comfort, peace, hope, and even beauty in the midst of it.

None of us journey far in this life without the waves of trial and heartache. As it says in Proverbs 14:10, "Each heart knows its own bitterness, and no one else can fully share its joy." I have wept beside many couples over the tragic death of a child. There are no words that can be spoken. I have come alongside many friends who are in the midst of loss almost beyond comprehension, when all I can offer is my love and presence and deep silent prayer. I have stood with many who've been ripped apart by addiction, imprisonment, or disease, and are seeking to sustain their hope.

Sometimes, just like with the Thundering Legion we looked at in chapter 9, suffering comes because we have given our lives to Jesus and chosen to be identified as his followers. We see this kind of suffering and oppression, persecution, and violence in our present world with greater frequency and in higher concentrations than perhaps any other time in human history. Once when I was visiting a ministry we work with in Nigeria, I shared a long discussion with students there who were studying and training for Christian ministry. The group I was meeting with came from various nations but shared in common that they had endured threats and even great emotional and physical abuse because they had become followers of Jesus. This happened because they were raised as Muslims in a land where it is illegal to convert to another faith. Their choice came with great consequences, including family rejection, prison, and threat of death. I was amazed as I heard these women and men share of how Jesus revealed himself directly to them in a vision or dream and how they were transformed by his love and gospel. I was also amazed by how these new friends all carried such joy and gratitude and hope even though they had endured much. I will never forget this.

I have often visited the nation of Liberia, where we are privileged to have ministries. Liberia is a nation that even prior to the recent devastation of the Ebola virus breakout had already suffered so deeply from a fifteen-year civil war. Enduring pain and loss has touched every family in this nation. One of our faithful elders and leaders in Liberia is a man named John. Through the years and waves of civil war, John remained faithful, often as a captive, on our mission in Po River. The mission was significantly destroyed by various rebel soldiers. But John remained there and kept alive the dream for the church, school, and medical mission to be fully rebuilt and restored.

During one visit with John, he spoke about some of what he had endured on the mission through those years. Then he said, "When you have suffered for something, you don't play with it anymore." John said that he had suffered for Jesus, and his Savior was so precious to him that he would never play games with him. He also expressed that the mission must be rebuilt, because he and others had suffered so greatly for it. It meant too much. I will never forget his words and the impact and wisdom they carried. (And—the mission is now being rebuilt!)

Sometimes walking with Jesus can simply be demanding and challenging. Jesus once described it like this: "The gateway to life is very narrow and the road is difficult" (Matthew 7:14). We may be misunderstood and mistreated and yet we are always called to do what is right even when it would seem so much easier not to.

If Jesus truly is God, then he has the right to ask us to make sacrifices in order to do what is right or best. In life, things often must be let go or left behind in order for other things to be picked up, and for us to move on. It is not always comfortable. Jesus understands; it was not always comfortable for him. He once described his journey to his followers like this:

> "The Son of Man must suffer many terrible things. . . . He will be rejected by the elders, the leading priests, and the teachers of religious law. He will be killed, but on the third day he will be raised from the dead."
>
> Then he said to the crowd, "If any of you wants to be my follower, you must turn from your selfish ways, take up your cross daily, and follow me. If you try to hang on to your life, you will lose it. But if you give up your life for my sake, you will save it." (Luke 9:22–24)

There is definitely sacrifice and risk on this journey with Jesus and the blue jeans gospel. But these are overwhelmed by the amazing reality of knowing Jesus and his forgiveness and peace and love. Even in the darkest moments, hope flickers—and we never walk alone.

In the early days of Jesus's life and ministry on earth, he was very popular. Everyone loved to be around him while he was healing and feeding people—each moment seemed filled with the miraculous. But then Jesus made it clear who he was and why he had come. The blue jeans gospel all of a sudden didn't feel quite as comfortable. Some didn't understand, some became angry, many turned away. In the midst of this, Jesus asked his closest friends and disciples if they were going to turn their backs on him and leave also. Peter said something profound and amazing. "Lord, to whom would we go? You have the words that give eternal life. We believe, and we know you are the Holy One of God" (John 6:68–69). That has remained a profound truth for me during the hard and gut-wrenching moments of life. There is nowhere else; there is no one else. Jesus is too real. He has suffered greatly for us and he never plays games with us. When the hard times come, he is there, and he is worthy.

··············· **REFLECTION** ···················

What thoughts emerge from what John said about Jesus and the Liberian mission, "When you suffer for something, you don't play with it anymore"? How does this connect to our current life and situation? What do we think about what Peter said?—"Lord, to whom would we go? You have the words that give eternal life. We believe, and we know you are the Holy One of God." What does it mean to live and wear the blue jeans gospel when it's not popular or comfortable?

Fourteen

...

EPILOGUE

Well, that's it. This book is a message from my heart to yours. Thanks for taking some time to read it. I'm simply trying to respond to God's heart and walk with him each day in faithfulness and integrity. I appreciate that you have joined me in the journey.

Jesus is so worthy. The gospel is so amazing. And blue jeans—well—that's just a reminder that walking with Jesus is meant to be real and natural—the place where our hearts are fully alive and our souls find comfort.

Life is very beautiful and very hard. Each day is a fresh opportunity to listen and respond to the Lord and to love, live, and serve for his glory. All around us are people who desperately need to know love, hear truth, and find hope. They are watching and listening and waiting. It's time to live real, put on those jeans, and reach up and reach out.

We never journey alone. Jesus is with us and will never leave or abandon us. And there are others who will walk with us. Remember, Christianity is a team sport—not a solo sport. Life goes by quickly and the seasons change. If Jesus is our Lord, the soon-arriving season will be one in which "God's home is now among his people! He will live with them, and they will be his people. God himself will be with them. He will wipe every tear from their eyes, and there will be no more death or sorrow or crying or pain. All these things are gone forever" (Revelation 21:3–4).

So let's keep walking and embracing the blue jeans gospel.

ABOUT THE AUTHOR

Rob Cruver is lead pastor of Zarephath Christian Church in Zarephath, New Jersey, where a growing number of people gather to love as Jesus loved, live as Jesus lived, and serve as Jesus served. Rob's sermons and "Go For It" messages can be heard on STAR 99.1 FM and its affiliate stations, and are also available online at www.zarephath.org. He is chancellor of Pillar College and executive director of Urban Impact. Rob also serves in leadership with The Pillar of Fire, which operates life-changing programs in many nations where he is privileged to travel. Rob holds graduate degrees in science, theology, and leadership. He and his wife, Debra, have two children. Rob's Levi's brand jeans get the most wear, and Debra likes her American Eagle Artist jeans best . . . this year.